# *M*AROON
# *T*EACHERS

# Maroon Teachers

## Teaching The Transatlantic Trade In Enslaved Africans

Sandra Ingrid Gift, PhD

Ian Randle Publishers
*Kingston • Miami*

First published in Jamaica, 2008 by
Ian Randle Publishers
11 Cunningham Avenue
Box 686
Kingston 6
www.ianrandlepublishers.com

© 2008 Sandra Ingrid Gift

ISBN 978-976-637-340-5 (pbk)

A catalogue record for this book is available from the National Library of Jamaica.

All rights reserved. No part of this publication may be reproduced, stored in a retrieval system or transmitted in any form or by any means electronic, photocopying, recording or otherwise, without the prior permission of the publisher and author.

Cover design by Gabby Woodham
Book design by Shelly-Gail Folkes

Printed in the United States of America

*For Stephan*

# TABLE OF CONTENTS

Preface and Acknowledgements / **viii**

Chapter 1: A Historical Overview of the Transatlantic Trade in Enslaved Africans and its Legacies / **1**

Chapter 2: Background and Conceptual Framework / **42**

Chapter 3: Issues and Challenges / **64**

Chapter 4: Teachers' Presentation of Content Knowledge / **81**

Chapter 5: Teachers' Organisation of Content Knowledge / **113**

Chapter 6: Emotional Dimensions / **145**

Chapter 7: Educational Significance / **165**

Chapter 8: Conclusion / **181**

Select Bibliography / **184**

Index / **191**

# Preface and Acknowledgements

This publication is based on my 2005 doctoral dissertation entitled 'Selected Teachers' Pedagogical Content Knowledge of the Transatlantic Slave Trade'. The publication was supported by a grant in 2006 from the University of the West Indies, St Augustine Campus' Research and Publication Fund and by the Gilder Lehrman Centre for Slavery, Resistance and Abolition at Yale University, where I was attached as a Research Affiliate in July 2006.

Two hundred years following the abolition of the Transatlantic Trade in Enslaved Africans (TTEA) secondary school teachers interviewed by the author must carve out for themselves and their students passages to freedom in the classroom context. The nature of these passages varies according to the extent to which the subject of the TTEA is seen as a legitimate area of study in the school curriculum. Through its Associated Schools Project Network (ASPnet) 'Transatlantic Slave Trade' Education Project, launched in 1998, the United Nations Educational Scientific and Cultural Organization (UNESCO) sought to break the silence surrounding the history of the TTEA and to locate the subject as an important area of study in secondary schools in those regions of the world that were involved in the trade. While this international educational platform facilitated secondary school teachers' deeper engagement of the subject, in the countries participating in the Project, several of them had to overcome contextual challenges to teach it. They had to discover creative means of circumventing the constraints of the official curriculum to enable their students to benefit as fully and in as meaningful a manner as possible from the opportunity to learn about the history of the TTEA and its impact on the societies in which they live. In their efforts to do so, they could be said to engage in 'educational marronage'. They are, therefore, in the eyes of this author, twenty-first century 'maroon teachers'. The challenges they confront to free themselves of the restrictions of their education systems might well reflect the challenges faced by many other teachers in teaching the TTEA. It is to teachers such as these 'maroon teachers' and others like them that we must turn as we seek to learn the lessons that we must apply if we are to succeed in the delivery of quality education on the subject of the TTEA.

It would not have been possible for me to undertake the research for this book without the invaluable and tremendously satisfying working experience which I enjoyed as Regional Coordinator for the UNESCO Associated Schools Project Network (ASPnet) 'Transatlantic Slave Trade (TST)' Education Project in the Caribbean and the Americas over the period 1998-2001. This Project was funded by the Norwegian Agency for Development Cooperation (NORAD). I am indebted to the ASPnet International Coordinator, Ms. Elizabeth Khawajkie, who entrusted me with this responsibility. Elizabeth retired from UNESCO on 31 January 2005 after a long and distinguished career with the organization. This publication is a reflection of the legacy of her contributions to the international community in the field of education. I acknowledge as well the members of the International Task Force who supported and guided the development of the Project.

I must express my heartfelt thanks to the teachers, administrators and students who agreed to be interviewed. With openness and trust they shared their rich experiences that have woven the fabric of the study on which this publication is based. To the core group of UNESCO ASPnet teachers in Trinidad and Tobago, I am especially indebted. I knocked on their doors which they never hesitated to open to me; I do cherish and thank them.

Professor Hilary Beckles, Caribbean historian; Principal of the Cave Hill Campus (Barbados) the University of the West Indies (UWI), and the representative of the Anglophone Caribbean on the International Task Force, proved to be a tremendous source of learning, insight and inspiration for me to deepen my own knowledge about the TTEA, its causes, consequences and legacies, and nurtured my appreciation of the great importance of the study of history.

Mr. Carol Keller, Caribbean teacher educator, and principal supervisor of my doctoral dissertation in the School of Education, UWI, engaged me in several sessions of intellectual exchange. I am extremely grateful to him for his guidance, perspicacity and collegiality, and for the benefit of the breadth and depth of his knowledge and understanding of education discourse.

Several other individuals expressed interest in and offered support for my research. I wish to acknowledge them. Professor Tony Martin, Caribbean historian, shared his research experience which proved very useful. Professor Bridget Brereton, Caribbean historian, read the first draft of my dissertation and provided detailed and valuable comments. My colleagues at the UWI School of Education, St Augustine campus, also kindly supported me with their invaluable feedback at various stages of the writing process. For this I thank especially Dr. Jeannette Morris, Dr. Jennifer Mohammed and Mrs. Janet Fullerton-Rawlins.

Professor Sylvia Frey, American historian, extended the hospitality of her home and office which made it possible for me to conduct interviews in New Orleans which helped, in no small way, to enrich the study. Professor Toni Walters, American higher education teacher educator, encouraged and guided me. Sonja Dumas and Jacqueline Moniquette assisted with proof reading and Anu Lakhan guided the final editing. Ms. Alysha Deonanan, cheerfully assisted in the typing of this manuscript. I acknowledge her competence and kind disposition, all of which made the task easier. I am grateful to them all for their generosity of spirit, and for their invaluable support.

I am deeply grateful to my parents Alfred and Sylvia Bushell for always being supportive of my goals. My husband, Professor Stephan Gift, and my sons, Allister and Christopher have had to live with my passion for this research, and with my mental and physical absences at those times that it consumed me. I thank them for their love, patience, tolerance, understanding and unconditional support. I have benefited from undertaking this investigation in ways both professional and personal. Finally, I thank Ian Randle for the publication of this book and Gabby Woodham for granting me permission to use his painting (title) on the cover.

My supervisors, advisors, supporters, family members and friends

*Preface and Acknowledgements* | *xi*

have contributed greatly to my academic and personal growth that ensured the completion of the research for this book. Any shortcomings, which may be perceived, however, are entirely my own responsibility.

Sandra Ingrid Gift

Chapter 1

# A Historical Overview of the Transatlantic Trade in Enslaved Africans (TTEA) and its Legacies

To begin to comprehend the significance of the teaching of the Transatlantic Trade in Enslaved Africans (TTEA), this Chapter examines some of the main ideas of the Enlightenment period in Western Europe as they relate to notions of human development. These include the ways in which the legacies of the trade have affected Atlantic societies, how some of these societies developed in the post-emancipation period, as well as issues relating to denial, shame, guilt, moral debt, trauma and institutionalized racism. Black people's identity and self-esteem and students' responses to the subject matter are also taken into account. The memorialization of the trade in enslaved Africans in the Americas and the Caribbean, Africa and Europe is briefly explored as the book treats with teachers' pedagogical content knowledge of the TTEA subject in these, the very regions which were part of the trade.

## The Historiography of the Transatlantic Trade in Enslaved Africans

For the purpose of teaching the TTEA, a major source of information for classroom teachers is historiography, either from primary or secondary sources. Arthur Marwick (1989, p.398) defines historiography as 'the systematic study of historians' interpretations of (or writings about) the past.' In this book, the term historiography is used as described by Mary Abbot (1996, p.112) as 'written history in general.'

The transatlantic trade in enslaved Africans is also referred to as the African/ or black slave trade. This was the trade in human beings from the sixteenth to the nineteenth century which linked, in economic and social ways, Europe, Africa and the Americas. The trade 'sustained a colossal colonial machine based on the slavery system' (Nelly Schmidt, 2004, p.61).

Walter Rodney (1972) argues that European capitalism set slavery and the Atlantic slave trade in motion, as Europe became the centre of a worldwide system. According to Rodney, the trade in human beings from Africa was brought about primarily by this and such like factors external to Africa. A principal initial factor was the demand for labour in Portugal and Spain and the Atlantic islands of São Tomé and the Canaries. In the Greater Antilles and the Spanish American mainland, the main demand came from mining and agricultural entrepreneurs. By the seventeenth century, the connections between European national economies and the wider world were well understood by European political economists. Rodney asserts that the commerce between Africa, England and the West Indies was seen as critical to England's development. For him, the high level of profits generated by the TTEA ensured its perpetuation over centuries. Europe's economic growth was stimulated and facilitated in various ways as a result of its supply of enslaved Africans. Sectors of the English economy which thrived on the TTEA at that time included trade, services, agriculture and manufacturing. He identifies the rise of seaport towns in Europe, in particular Bristol, Liverpool, Nantes, Bordeaux and Seville, as the most spectacular feature in European development, all linked with the African trade. The emergence of manufacturing centres facilitated the Industrial Revolution. Rodney argues that Europe's trade connection with Africa contributed not only to Europe's economic development but also to its real development in terms of its increased capacity for growth and independence. As in Europe, profits from slavery and the slave trade in the American colonies were invested in commercial ports and industrial areas. The time came in Europe, however, when the leading capitalist states determined that the TTEA and the use of enslaved labour in the Americas was not in the interest of Europe's continuing development.

Rodney comments on the effects of ties with Africa on the

development of ideas within European capitalist society. According to Rodney the most striking feature of these effects of the thinking in Europe was the rise of racism that was widespread and deeply rooted. Rodney notes that slavery's role in the promotion of racial prejudice and ideology has been carefully examined, particularly in the USA. He asserts that white racism emerged as an essential aspect of the capitalist mode of production of which the Atlantic slave trade was an integral part. Following Eric Williams' thesis in *Capitalism and Slavery* he also argues that it was primarily for economic rather than racist reasons that European planters and miners enslaved Africans in the Americas. The opening up of the New World for wealth generation would have been impossible without African labour. The exploitation of African people on racist grounds 'accompanied, strengthened and became indistinguishable from oppression for economic reasons' (Rodney1972 in Shepherd and Beckles, 2000, p.10).

Robin Blackburn (1999) indicates that European systems of colonial slavery in the Americas were highly commercialized so that from the sixteenth to the nineteenth centuries the Atlantic trade became the 'pacemaker of global exchanges' (Blackburn, 1999, p.3). The commercial plantation commodities were mainly tobacco, sugar and cotton, grown by the enslaved Africans for new and expanding patterns of consumption in Europe, which contrasted with the meagre rations and self-provision of the enslaved peoples. The colonial enterprise was based on a seemingly sophisticated system of technical and economic organization (Blackburn, 1999).

## ENSLAVED NOT SLAVES

The term 'enslaved' is used to refer to the condition and process of enslavement to which Africans were subjected with the coming of the Europeans. The use of this term is informed by the view that enslaved Africans ought not to be seen as intrinsically embodying the status of slaves, but as persons who were systematically enslaved for the purpose of the colonial project. The process of enslavement was institutional and sustained for more than 300 years resulting in socio-cultural legacies which continue to challenge the people of Africa and its diaspora.

The emphasis here, is on the active process of enslavement rather than on social categorization. Beverly Tatum (1992) makes the point that racial categories were originally created to service oppression and their sustained use is a continuation of oppression. The discussion of a problematic and flawed social construct is difficult without the use of the problematic language.

## Slavery

Orlando Patterson (1982) examines slavery using contexts of personal relations with power structures. Enslaved persons were permanently and violently dominated. For Patterson, slavery, as one of the most extreme forms of domination, facilitated the total power of the slave owner over the enslaved person. Three facets of the power relation were: (i) the use or threat of violence in the control of a person; (ii) psychologically persuading a group to alter how they viewed their interests and circumstances; and (iii) culturally transforming 'force into right and obedience into duty' (Patterson, 1982, p.2). He underscores the extent to which brute force served as the basis of the master-slave relationship. Patterson suggests the enslaved person had no being without the slave owner and socially existed only through the slave owner. The slave, therefore, became institutionally 'a social non-person'.

The enslaved person was socially excommunicated and this was achieved by the denial of claims on, and obligations to, parents and living blood relations as well as ancestors and descendants. The isolation brought about by African enslavement was, therefore, also genealogical. The condition of enslavement thus entailed cultural isolation from the social heritage of ancestors. While enslaved persons had a past, this was not a heritage. Enslaved Africans did not enjoy the freedom of integrating ancestral experience into their lives, of using their natural forbears' inherited meanings to inform their understanding of social reality or of anchoring '...the living present in any conscious community of memory' (Patterson, 1982, p.5).

The absence of formal recognition of the social relations of enslaved persons had serious emotional and social implications. According to Paul Lovejoy (2000) special features of slavery included the concept of enslaved persons as property; as outsiders because of their origins or because of having been denied their heritage as a result of legal or other penalties; the use of coercion; the slave owner having considerable control over the enslaved person's labour power, sexuality and reproductive capacities. Further, the slave status was one that was inherited until modified.

Certain characteristics typified individual slave systems. Lovejoy identifies broad patterns which served to distinguish slavery from other forms of exploitation. It was almost always through the use of violence that a person's status of being free and being a citizen was reduced to the condition of slavery. The slave was an instrument of labour and could be forced to comply with orders. The violence of slavery was inescapable and dialectically, it produced 'both a psychology of servility and the potential for rebellion' (Lovejoy, 2000, p.7). Unless the slave owner consented, the enslaved could not marry in the Christian church. Their offspring were not legally their own but the property of the slave owner, thus male slaves were denied legal paternity over their children.

Lovejoy indicates that slavery in the Americas exhibited many features similar to slavery of other periods and in other places. In addition to the extent of the physical violence and the degree of psychological force used to control the enslaved Africans, the features of slavery included the holding of enslaved persons in large economic units known as plantations, and the significant numbers of enslaved Africans. This notwithstanding, two features distinguish the system as it pertains to the TTEA: (i) the use of racial ideologies to control the enslaved population and (ii) the developed economic rationalization of the system that was tied to the production of staple commodities for global trade.

In the introduction to his book *Slavery and Human Progress*, Brion David Davis (1984) summarizes two theories relating to slavery and economic progress. He describes the first category of theories as belonging to fundamentalist Marxian wisdom that is classic and liberal. This category of theories accepts that, while one may understand slavery as 'a stage in human evolution' (Davis, 1984, p.xiii) slavery always hindered technological innovation and social and economic growth. The second category of theories to which Davis refers holds that nineteenth-century technology, high growth rates and slavery were compatible, and that slavery was abolished 'when its contribution to western capitalism was just beginning to matter' (p.xiv). While the first category of theories implies that historical progress and impersonal laws would naturally bring about the demise of slavery, and that economic progress would bring improvements both socially and morally, Davis indicates that the second category of theories raises questions concerning the economic reasons behind emancipation and the forms of labour which took the place of plantation slavery.

Davis further separates these two categories of theories into four different arguments. These arguments seem to have implications for the interpretation of abolition or emancipation. The first argument came from social theorists, from the time of the eighteenth century, from scholars and philosophers such as John Millar, Auguste Comte, Karl Marx and Frederick Engels, as well as from several evangelical Christian abolitionists. They considered slavery 'a necessary but primitive stage in the evolution of human institutions' (p.xiv).

Davis describes the second argument as a variant of the first. This is the Williams school. These writers held the view that the enslavement of Africans by Europeans was necessary for Europeans engaged in the conquering and settling of the New World, and in the accumulation of capital for the financing of the Industrial Revolution. They argue that it was at the expense of the enslaved Africans that European modern capitalism was built. When it was considered that enslaved labour was no longer economical and was no longer supportive of capitalist development, it was deemed 'unprogressive' by capitalists and they abolished it. Davis states that the Williams school did not imply any moral justification for the necessity of African enslavement for Western progress.

The third argument was provided by abolitionists and classical economists. They saw slave labour as necessarily retarding both sustainable economic growth and social and moral progress. 'The underlying assumption was that oppressors cannot violate the immutable laws of nature without paying a heavy price' (Davis, Brion, 1984, p.xv). This point of view featured prominently in American historiography. It was believed by a large number of historians that black slavery was a fatal incentive to labour, technological innovation and the desire for the improvement of self.

The fourth argument is opposed to the third argument. In its most extreme form, it advanced the view that slavery was a progressive institution in terms of economic benefits; one under which the average enslaved person in the field benefited by enjoying in her or his lifetime the greater part of the income they generated. While such views have been disputed by economists and historians, Davis states that subsequent scholarship tended to give them credence. The ongoing controversy around this issue has made scholars reluctant to refer to a slave system as necessarily 'becoming "moribund" or being doomed to "inevitable decline" (Davis, 1984, p .xvi).

## THE NEW SLAVERY

Kevin Bales in his publication *Disposable People, New Slavery in the Global Economy* (2000) reminds us, lest we forget, that slavery has not ended; that it is not a horror that has been consigned safely to the past. Modern slavery is characterized by the existence of slaveholders, as opposed to slave owners, since, while there is no legal ownership of human beings, those who buy people today do nonetheless gain control over them and employ violence to maintain their control. The new forms of slavery continue, therefore, to be a means of human underdevelopment. Describing modern slavery as an enterprise that is illegal and shadowy, thus rendering it difficult to arrive at reliable statistics, Bales estimates the number of enslaved persons in the world today to be about 27 million, a much smaller number than that advanced by some activists who indicate a figure of 200 million. Enslaved persons can be found in almost any country, including the most developed.

Today's enslaved persons are generally used to meet simple, non-technological and traditional labour requirements. Large international corporations, with subsidiaries in the developing world also benefit from the labour of enslaved persons to increase their profits. Race is not a significant factor in the new slavery; rather vulnerability is. The criteria for enslavement today focus on weakness, gullibility and deprivation, not colour, tribe, or religion. Modern slaveholders are described as predators who prey on weaknesses and who rapidly adapt '...an ancient practice to the new global economy'(Bales, 2000, p.11).

Today, access to enslaved persons is considered cheap. Slaves no longer represent a major investment; slaveholders exhaust their usefulness and then discard them. Since they cost so little, securing permanent 'legal' ownership of them brings no added value and thus they are disposable. While there is enormous variation in the length of time an enslaved person spends in bondage, in modern slavery most enslaved persons are held temporarily; some only for a few months as it is not profitable to keep them once their immediate usefulness has ceased. Bales points to the key differences between the old and new slavery, indicated below:

| Old Slavery | New Slavery |
| --- | --- |
| Legal ownership asserted | Legal ownership avoided |
| High purchase cost | Very low purchase cost |
| Low profits | Very high profits |
| Shortage of potential slaves | Surplus of potential slaves |
| Long-term relationship | Short-term relationship |
| Slaves maintained | Slaves disposable |
| Ethnic differences important | Ethnic differences not important |

(Bales, 2000, p.15)

## The TTEA as a Phenomenon in World History

Scholars in the Caribbean and beyond have been examining the TTEA as a phenomenon in world history for over 100 years. There is a rich tradition of interpretation of this trade within the Caribbean and in the wider world. From as early as 1804, when the state of Haiti was declared by the formerly enslaved persons who wrote their constitution, the view was set out that slavery was a crime against humanity and that all human beings aspire to freedom, thereby registering the Caribbean intellectual tradition and strong objection to slavery and the TTEA.

John Jacob Thomas, C.L.R. James and Eric Williams are among the early scholars who examined the trade as a phenomenon in world history. Michael Manley, Caribbean intellectual, leader and a former prime minister of Jamaica, in Cateau and Carrington (2000), makes the point that in the nineteenth and early twentieth centuries Caribbean people were at the mercy of 'a history of perceived injustice' without the benefit of the means of understanding how that history had been shaped. Eric Williams launched his seminal thesis, *Capitalism and Slavery* in this uncertain historical landscape. For Manley, the analysis underpinning Williams's thesis challenged traditional thinking to shed light on historical truth.

The perceptions of Caribbean people of their history and their location within it were redefined in *Capitalism and Slavery*. Collectively, Williams's books are recognized as forming an important contribution to Caribbean historiography. The impact of his work was both intellectual and political. Colin Palmer, Caribbean historian, in Cateau and Carrington (2000), applauds Williams for his uncompromising challenge of the paradigms used for the writing of history. Modern scholars have built upon this tradition, thus producing a rich historiography on all aspects of what is now agreed was a human tragedy.

Walter Rodney (1972), in his examination of Europe's dominance of the worldwide trade system, emphasizes the dialectical relationship between development and underdevelopment, and notes that 'the two help produce each other by interaction' (Rodney, 1972 in Shepherd and Beckles, 2000, p.1). He states that for four and a half centuries, going back to the fifteenth century, the developed and underdeveloped parts of the capitalist world had been in continuous contact, and over this period Africa contributed to the development of Western Europe to the same degree that Western Europe contributed to Africa's underdevelopment.

The TTEA was a global event with significant economic, political, and cultural impact on the Atlantic world and beyond. Blackburn (1999) describes the Atlantic slave trade as being responsible for the establishment of one of the largest systems of slavery in human history; one that was very significant given the businesslike principles which informed its conduct, its scale and destructiveness. Commenting on the reality that enslaved Africans met their own subsistence needs over one or two days' work per week and laboured for the slave owners the remainder of the time, he states that the rate of exploitation of the enslaved Africans had few parallels, even among other slave systems.

Director General of UNESCO, Koïchiro Matsuura, in a message

observing the United Nations International Year to Commemorate the Struggle against Slavery and its Abolition in 2004, described the TTEA and slavery as constituting one of the darkest chapters in the history of the world, given its duration, its extensiveness, and its consequences. UNESCO estimates that the trans-Saharan trade in enslaved Africans, (conducted primarily by the Arabs from the seventh to the nineteenth centuries in Africa, the Mediterranean and the Indian Ocean) transported about 12 million people, while the TTEA deported between 15 and 18 million enslaved Africans in a shorter time.

Olu Oguibe (2001), Nigerian artist and author and Livio Sansone (2001), Italian anthropologist, refer to the TTEA as a phenomenon in world history. Randall Robinson (2000), African-American writer and activist, describes this trade as the black holocaust, and considers it the most heinous human rights crime to have been suffered by any group of people in the world over the past 500 years, in particular because of its enduring legacies. He writes, 'It is a human rights crime without parallel in the modern world. For it produces its victims ad infinitum, long after the active stage of the crime has ended'(p.216). In the case of the USA, he states, slavery was extended by government-sponsored segregation and racial discrimination against blacks by more than a century.

Oguibe sees the TTEA as a unique event in the history of the human species, with no rival in world history in 'epochal monumentality, chronological spread, or sustained cruelty' (Oguibe in Oostindie 2001, p.95). He explains that the theme and historical event of the trade continue to preoccupy the imagination of the world beyond Africa and its diaspora. Within and across race and ethnicity, the enduring memory of slavery is manifest in the everyday world of music and visual culture, literature, religious traditions and in social, economic and political relations.

For Oguibe, the central feature of the grand epic of the African sojourn in the Western world is chattel enslavement and the inhumanity of the Middle Passage experience. He attributes the persistence of memory, of guilt and shame around slavery to the devastation of 'entire peoples and cultures, the psychic scar of a horrific journey away from the familiar and across the bottomless sea to centuries of brutal subjugation and disenfranchisement'

(Oguibe, in Oostindie 2001, p.96). He argues that a chasm exists between those who have inherited this legacy, descendants of the slave owner and descendants of the enslaved, which time has not been able to fill. The phenomenon TTEA is perpetuated in the accompanying anxiety it generates and in its continuing palpability as a lived experience that re-stimulates the present.

Sansone (2001) states that the TTEA was a transnational phenomenon which resulted in suffering, dehumanization and racialization at a universal level. It spanned the regions of the 'Black Atlantic' which include the tropical lowlands of the Pacific coast of Central and Latin America. He observes, however, that its transnational character notwithstanding, the memory of slavery, surprisingly, is defined by characteristics that are local, based on relations, and that are part of wider circumstances.

James Horton (2006), African American historian, underscores the importance of enslaved Africans to the American economy. He argues that they were a central part of the American economy as demonstrated in 'the tobacco plantations of the Chesapeake or the rice fields of Carolina, as cargo in slave ships fitted out in New England or as trade items financed by the merchants of New York and Pennsylvania'(p.38).

## THE AGE OF ENLIGHTENMENT

Nelly Schmidt (2004), French researcher, connects the ideas of the leading figures of the Age of Enlightenment in Western Europe in the mid eighteenth century, to the idea of slavery as a crime against humanity. Marie-Jean-Antoine-Nicolas de Caritat, Marquis de Condorcet, in his *Réflexions sur L'esclavage des Nègres*, published in 1781 described the reduction of a human being; slavery ' to buying, selling and keeping a human being in servitude 'as a crime worse than theft (the theft of private property in capitalism being regarded as a crime of great proportion). Charles de Secondat, Baron de Brčde et de Montesquieu writing his *Esprit des Lois* in 1748, passed judgement on slavery as being 'against nature' and *The Encyclopédie* (published under the direction of Denis Diderot as a massive reference work for the arts and sciences and to propagate the ideas of the French Enlightenment), expressed the wish that, rather than make so many miserable, the European colonies should be destroyed. In 1756, François Marie Arouet Voltaire, in his *Essai sur Les Moeurs*, expressed surprise that civil rights in Europe were being discussed at a time when the lives of enslaved Africans were being compromised to flatter Europeans' new appetites.

The *Histoire Philosophique et Politique des Etablissements et du Commerce des Européens dans les Deux Indes*, a collective work published in 1770 under the name of the Abbé Raynal, served to further enhance critical European opinion on the question of slavery and human rights.

Within the English tradition, Thomas Clarkson and William Wilberforce were anti-slavery advocates. According to Schmidt, it was they who inspired the founders of the Société des Amis des Noirs et des Colonies in 1796 which followed the establishment in Paris in 1788 of the Société des Amis des Noirs. The founders of these societies called for a ban on the black slave trade at the time. While abuses of authority by slave owners and the ill-treatment of the enslaved Africans were condemned, the slavery system was not economically reappraised, even though in 1776 Adam Smith pointed out that, in general, free labour was superior to enslaved labour since the force of the whip does not produce in people intelligence, zeal or inventiveness.

Rodney (1972) noted the contradiction between the elaboration of democratic ideas within Europe, and Europeans' authoritarian and brutal practices in regard to Africans. The ideals of 'Liberty, Equality and Fraternity' of the French Revolution were not seen as extending to Africans enslaved by France in the West Indies and the Indian Ocean. Instead, France resisted their efforts for their self-emancipation and, according to Rodney (1972), the leaders of the Revolution declared that their efforts were not on behalf of black humanity. In the USA as well, despite the American constitution declaring in its preamble the equality of all men, the continued enslavement of Africans was sanctioned.

## LEGACIES OF SLAVERY

The legacies of the TTEA as they relate to human development in Africa, the Americas/Caribbean and Europe are reflective of the local variants of the impact of the trade.

The specific legacies and human development issues revolve around the following: (i) education, memory, denial, shame, guilt and moral debt; (ii) trauma and institutionalized racism; (iii) black people's self-esteem and identity; and (iv) memorialization of the trade. Since it is not possible to treat with these issues in an exhaustive manner, selected local variants of these legacies are presented. The discussion of education, memory, denial, shame, guilt and moral debt focuses on the three regions (Africa, the Americas/Caribbean, Europe); trauma and institutionalized racism are considered with reference to the African-American situation; issues of identity and self-esteem are examined in the context of in the English-speaking Caribbean; and memorialization TTEA is considered briefly in the contexts of Africa, Brazil and the USA.

## LEGACIES IN EDUCATION AND OF MORAL DEBT

Marika Sherwood (1998), author and senior research fellow at the Institute of Commonwealth Studies, points out that for students in the UK, after the age of 14, history is not a compulsory subject on the national curriculum. Rather, whether or not students do history seems to depend upon the schools' choice of examination board. Even though the 14 and over syllabi are broader than those for younger students, it remains Eurocentred. While this is presumed reasonable in a European nation, it nonetheless raises questions of the meaningfulness of such syllabi for youths of non-European heritage in the British school system, and what all youth are learning about those of non-European ancestry.

Sherwood argues that the school and the curriculum are possible sources of alienation of youths in the UK who are not of European heritage; that this is linked to the issue of whose history is being taught and to the absence of black history in UK history textbooks. According to Sherwood, UK history textbooks fail to reasonably deal with the presence of Caribbean immigrants in the country. Africa too, either remained absent from texts used for history in schools or was distorted, ignored or denigrated, and it is only upon the entry of the white man that the *tabula rasa* of Africa becomes pencilled in. Even textbooks recognized as 'good' were known to present stereotypic images of Asians and Africans as being inevitably and rightly subject to European government and interests. She makes the point that the concept of civilization is subject to manipulation by subjectivity and prejudice and that this is likely to influence the teaching of history.

Though the revised mandatory national curriculum in history facilitates a broader interpretation of the history indicated in study units, only teachers willing to work on their own undertake this. Sherwood is critical of what she describes as the 'senseless' approach of formatting texts so that they abound with illustrations, thus reducing to a minimum the amount of reading required.

The Black and Asian Studies Association was established in 1991 in the UK. Sherwood offers no definition of 'black' but throughout her writing the issues raised relate to Africans, West Indians and Asians who have historically lived in the UK. A key activity of the Association in this regard was the investigation of schools' textbooks' content.

Some of the findings of this investigation reveal that while the UK National History Curriculum required that students be taught about 'the social, cultural, religious and ethnic diversity of societies studied' (Sherwood, 1998, p.18) in reality such diversities were, in general, excluded from the texts. Since such instruction is not inspected, it is not taught. From the history taught in the UK it is expected that students' 'moral judgement' will be refined but that history should not lead them to 'chew over past glories or, even worse, past resentments and guilts' (Sherwood, 1998, p.19).

Harry Goulbourne (2001), Jamaican professor of sociology in London, argues that Britain's collective national consciousness about slavery is its proud record in leading the crusade to end the trade in enslaved Africans in 1807. This pride embraces the humanitarian and noble efforts of Clarkson and Wilberforce, the eventual abolition of slavery between 1834 and 1838 and the British navy's policing the high seas against those nations that persisted with the trade. The British national sense of rectitude, in contrast with the attempts of Napoleonic France to reintroduce slavery in the West Indies and, in particular, in Haiti, continues to inform its national psyche. Nonetheless, relatively little action has been taken to 'address or redress the monumental injustice of African slavery across the Atlantic world' (Goulbourne in Oostindie 2001 p.127).

Referring to the efforts, through the establishment of museums and galleries, for example, to re-awaken in the national consciousness Britain's past involvement in the transatlantic trade in enslaved Africans, Goulbourne deems these to be inadequate as a recognition of a past that is shameful and which continues to overshadow the present. He states that there has been no exorcising of guilt in Britain with the ending of slavery as has happened for the defenders of apartheid in South Africa.

On the other hand, in a discussion of slavery, truth and reconciliation in the UK, James Walvin (2001), professor of history at the University of York, UK, makes the point that films like *Amistad*, novels like Toni Morrison's *Beloved* and television series such as *Roots* (based on Alex Haley's novel) have hastened the process of increased public awareness of slavery. This process has also been confirmed by the recent demand for reparations for slavery, advocated by the Nairobi based Organisation for African Unity. Prominent spokespersons of the black community in Britain have adopted these demands. Several significant events and innovations have pushed forward demands for a reassessment of Britain's past. In this regard, a major breakthrough was the decision to locate a permanent exhibition of the trade at the Liverpool Maritime Museum in 1996. Walvin, who was guest curator for this exhibition, reports that the establishment of the exhibition became a reality, notwithstanding many problems and objections from local resource groups. The exhibition proved to be a great success with large numbers of appreciative visitors having the opportunity to view it.

Given the enduring legacies of the transatlantic trade in enslaved Africans which include denial, ambiguity, shame and guilt, Robinson (2001), focusing on the status of African Americans, calls for setting afoot 'a new and whole black woman and man'(p.7); he makes a call for telling the victims of this trade what happened to them.

Doudou Diène (2001), retired director of UNESCO's Slave Route Project, reflecting on the magnitude of the conspiracy that lay behind the African slave trade is of the view that all those who took part and who were in agreement or said nothing against it, owe a moral debt. Jean-Michel Deveau (2001), French historian, acknowledges that it is only now that the silence shrouding the written history of the trade is being lifted. Like Diène (2001), he reiterates that the subject of the TTEA is brushed aside both in Europe and Africa. He explains that it is broached with reluctance in school textbooks which perpetuate clichés and do not take account of recent research findings. Deveau (2001) states that it is only in the past 20 years or so that Europeans have started to study the TTEA with a scientific approach, and very few specialists on the subject exist. At the time of writing, Deveau notes that in France, there were only about ten university theses on the subject with two or three others in preparation. Further, he explains, the silence about the TTEA is observed in curricula which avoid a clear treatment of the past. In textbooks, the events of the trade are 'dodged, portrayed in a biased manner or simply glossed over' (Deveau in Diène (2001) p.401). Nonetheless, because there does exist a general awareness of what happened, school children conclude that the denials of the facts or the 'half-confessions' really reveal a sense of shame that is inherited as '...an integral part of the national heritage?'

Deveau (2001) also observes a heavy silence about the TTEA in Africa and declares that the entire history of the continent is still to be written. He makes the following points: (i) the internal history of the different forms of slave-trading in Africa was still to be sketched; (ii) young African historians now acknowledge that the continent of Africa itself carried a significant part of the responsibility for the transatlantic trade, although this was not widely admitted; (iii) this aspect of the subject represents a very big research area that was opening up; (iv) teachers face a dilemma in teaching the subject which seems to be prone to manipulation based on particular interests at a given point in time.

Deveau wonders how teachers can find their way in their teaching given the vulnerability of history to manipulation — and given that the subject of the transatlantic trade in enslaved Africans generates reservations and can even disappear as a result of ignorance. He proposes as an important way forward the inclusion of factual information about the trade in school curricula.

Robinson (2001) asserts that in every competitive society the dominant group, consciously or unconsciously, uses instruction in history and the humanities to sustain its primacy, whether or not this has been ill-gotten.

James Horton (2006) advocates greater knowledge and understanding of this important part of American history to facilitate meaningful conversations about race in the USA in the twenty-first century. According to Horton, most people in the USA do not know enough about the history of slavery to enable them to contribute intelligently to national discussions on the subject. Further, some people would prefer not to know and it is only recently that opportunities have been provided for learning about the subject. Traditionally, there has been little mention of slavery in textbooks in the USA and public schools in the North were virtually silent about it. While in the segregated South black schools generally included some information about it, Southern white schools were silent on the subject. Horton states that in these schools any meagre treatment of the subject was presented as a problem that emerged on the eve of the Civil War.

Public school curricula often communicated the pro-slavery propaganda of slavery as a benevolent system designed in keeping with black people's intellectual and social limitations. This propaganda continued to be influential beyond the nineteenth century. Generally, textbooks reinforced the romantic and sentimental portrayals of slavery in popular novels and films 'casting slaves as childlike creatures who often exasperated lovingly benign white masters' (p.40).

Public education ensured that children thought about slavery and race in ways that would reinforce twentieth-century American law and custom assumptions of white supremacy. Representations in popular culture confirmed these assumptions for adults. The nineteenth-century anti-slavery novel *Uncle Tom's Cabin* by Harriet Beecher Stowe and the twentieth-century southern romantic novel *Gone with the Wind* by Margaret Mitchell and its film adaptation provided the 'contradictory views upon which most American beliefs about slavery are based' (p.41). Stowe condemned the institution of slavery but her depiction of the enslaved nonetheless paralleled that of Mitchell's portrayal of the servant who was lovable but limited and that was consistent with portrayals of slavery in many twentieth-century textbooks. To varying degrees, writes Horton, most Americans growing to maturity before the mid 1960s carry this picture of slavery with them. This socialization shaped their racial opinions which, consciously or subconsciously, most expect to have confirmed at visits to public history sties or museums.

Recent scholarship has influenced changes in the content of many textbooks used in college and in a few used in the public secondary schools in the USA in the last two generations. The best accounts of American history now include slavery and the role of race more generally, though this is sometimes in a limited form. Still, in part because much of the best and latest scholarship almost never reaches high school teachers, this scholarship never reaches high school students. Shedding light on 'this alarming situation' (p.42), Horton cites a United States Department of Education study of public school history teaching in the mid 1990s which found that, in most high schools, teachers with inadequate training in history taught history courses. The situation is further aggravated in many public schools where history courses have been shortened or removed entirely from the curriculum. Knowledge of American history is often limited even among the most educated in the USA and their understanding of slavery is often stereotypical or nonexistent (p.42). The Federal government's concerns about the quality of education in public schools have resulted in government-sponsored and privately funded grant programmes to address the quality of education in public schools and this includes teaching American history. In the mid 1990s, the Gilder Lehrman Institute of American History began funding summer seminars for public school teachers. The Institute also provided significant assistance for establishing 'History High Schools, public schools with a focus on American history' (p.43.) The seminars are now taught to hundreds of teachers, at more than a dozen institutions across the USA, by some of the most prominent American scholars. Because of these important public and private teacher education programmes, the history of slavery is beginning to make its way into American public schools.

At the international level, UNESCO has also sought to break the silence surrounding the TTEA by addressing the moral debt with the launch in 1998 of the UNESCO Associated Schools Project Network

(ASPnet) 'Transatlantic' Slave 'Trade' (TST) Education Project involving a number of secondary schools in the three regions that were involved in the trade: Africa, the Americas/Caribbean and Europe. The TST Education Project which was originally supported with funding from the Norwegian Agency for Development (NORAD) serves as the educational arm of UNESCO's Slave Route Project. With the cessation of this funding however, the continuation of this project lies in peril.

## MEMORY AND HISTORY

Given the long history of the brutal system of human exploitation in the region it is not surprising that slavery survives in the collective consciousness of Caribbean people. Bernard Bailyn (2001) points out that the issue of living memory calls forth a distinction between history and memory.

Bailyn (2001) acknowledges that in the historiography of the TTEA there is an important place for numbers and simple quantities since a sense of magnitude can facilitate understanding. He points out, however, that even though the brutality, inhumanity and devastation of the trade is known, it is harder to face its clinical and accurate analysis. Confronted with the details of the transatlantic trade in enslaved Africans, objectivity is possible only up to a certain point. Beyond this point we become emotionally involved (pp. 249-250).

Since the story of enslaved Africans exists in living memory — and not only for people of African heritage — all are morally implicated to some degree and must contemplate the association of history with memory. Bailyn observes that the problematic relationship between history and memory has until recently been discussed mainly in connection with the holocaust in which six million Jews were exterminated during the Second World War. The subject of the holocaust is constantly analyzed in *History and Memory*, the journal that was founded to document the recollection of the holocaust which is still part of living memory. According to Bailyn, historiography is source-bound reconstruction of past events, circumstances, and people; a reconstruction that is critical, sceptical, empirical and based on the belief that the past is both distant from us and different.

Historians are said to avoid projecting the past into the present, seeking instead to explain events 'for their own sakes and in their own terms' (Bailyn 2001, p.250).

Historians, therefore, use available documentation to shed light on the outcomes which those in the past did not know but which today are known. This is approached in a manner that is critical and sceptical out of an awareness that it is not possible to recreate the past in all its elements. With this in mind, historians establish a distance between themselves and the past and the telling of stories, aware that emerging facts will change the stories being told; that other perspectives can change the historian's focus and that other interpretations can provoke a reconsideration of the story.

Memory, on the other hand, does not reconstruct the past critically or with scepticism. Rather it is:

> the spontaneous unquestioned experience of the past. It is absolute, not tentative or distant, and it is expressed in signs and signals, symbols, images and mnemonic clues of all sorts. It shapes our awareness whether we know it or not, and it is ultimately emotional, not intellectual (Bailyn, 2001, p.50).

It is not possible to reduce the memory of the TTEA to an alien context. The memory of the trade is not a reconstruction that is critical or rational. It is not distant. It is a vicarious experience that is living and immediate (Bailyn, 2001, p.250). That memory is buried in the people's consciousness, shaping their view of the world, and they are surrounded by its sites, symbols and clues. Bailyn states:

> It is the Middle Passage that every child reads about in textbooks. It is evoked in Alex Hayley's Roots and Steven Spielberg's Amistad – which are less history than memory… It lies barely below the surface in every discussion of race relations in public policy (Bailyn, 2001, p.250).

Such collective memory is inescapable and cannot be distanced by a rational and critical reconstruction of the past. It is immediate, urgent and emotional and cannot be constrained by scholarship.

David Blight (2006), American historian, indicates that historians now justifiably use the lens of "memory" to study the past as they have come to understand that diverse peoples employ the "myths" by which they live to define themselves. Blight addresses the issue of what distinguishes history from memory describing them as representing 'two antagonistic attitudes toward the past' (p.5) that must at some point converge and collaborate. For Blight, historians discover and preserve the facts and stories behind people's imagining of their civic lives. History roots itself in research and reason to reconstruct the past; with a tendency to be critical and sceptical of people's motives and actions. It is also more 'relative, contingent on place, chronology, scale, and multiple causation' (p.5).

Memory, on the other hand, identifies itself as a set of meanings and stories that is sacred, absolute and held as a community's heritage or identity. While memory is frequently owned, history is interpreted. Memory is transmitted across generations but history undergoes revisions with each generation. Monuments, objects or sites are the means by which memory coalesces while the understanding of contexts in all their complexity is the goal of history. The essence of history constitutes academic training and evidence but memory conveys the immediacy and 'authority of community membership and experience' (p.5). Horton, nonetheless, makes the point that is very difficult for historians to be completely objective. These distinguishing features notwithstanding, both history and memory are essential to transmitting the past and teachers and historians have a valuable role to play in disseminating information about the past to young people.

Randall Robinson (2000) African American activist also emphasizes the importance of memory. For him, living successfully and triumphantly needs to be informed by a strong memory of the past. He cites the example of Haitian culture which, he states, has retained more of its Africanness than Black American culture and which serves as a compelling statement of the power of memory.

## Memorialization of the Transatlantic Trade in Enslaved Africans

Gert Oostindie (2001) presents the perspectives of contemporary researchers and writers on the commemoration of slavery in the publication *Facing up to the Past*. The publication presents a wide variety of perspectives principally from the Americas, but also from Africa and Europe, though to a lesser degree. Several of the articles analyze how slavery is commemorated or expunged from public memory in particular places. It also discusses the trifling value of some official gestures at memorializing the trade, and the ways in which artists and educational institutions confront the subject, inter alia. The views of the following contributors to this publication, that is, Oostindie (2001) are discussed in this section: Ama Ata Aidoo (Ghana), Olu Oguibe (Nigeria), Hilary McD Beckles (Barbados), Allison Blakely (USA), Seymour Drescher (USA), Harry Goulbourne (Jamaica), Achille Mbembe (Cameroon), James Walvin (UK), Flávio dos Santos Gomes (Brazil), and Livio Sansone (Italy).

The discussion is approached from a geographic perspective.

### Africa

British historian James Walvin (2001), refers to the subject of the trade in enslaved Africans as standing out as a dark and violent theme in African history, going back more than 400 years. The spectre of slavery continues to haunt African consciousness. Achille Mbembe (2001), Cameroonian historian and author, views the Atlantic slave trade, more than the trans-Saharan slave trade, as the principal symbol of the suffering of black people historically. He identifies a paradigm of victimization as being almost always evident in the discourse about Africa. This notwithstanding, the paradox exists that the Atlantic slave trade is generally not recognized as being of any significance by most Africans. Further, Mbembe argues, the Atlantic slave trade, the Arab slave trade, and indigenous forms of servitude have not served as platforms for the re-organization of the social bond, for an African philosophy of life and a means of participating in the world. Colonization and apartheid have been used to mask slavery around which silence still prevails.

Slavery is considered to have resulted in the humiliation, degradation and torment of Africans who are also seen as having experienced social death. Mbembe (2001) describes as the manifestations of social death a denial of dignity, dispersion and suffering of exile. He asserts that there is no African memory of slavery or, if one exists, it is fragmented. Further, in Africa, debates about African slavery are viewed as seeking to evoke feelings of guilt while ignoring responsibility for the past, yet giving the impression of addressing the issue. Efforts to consciously recall slavery have met with ambivalence.

Elisée Soumonni (2001), historian from Benin, explains that the subject is a difficult one because of its sensitive and emotive dimension. It is still taboo on the African continent. This is so despite the growing interest in its study and despite the widespread occurrence of modern forms of slavery. The focus is generally on the African diaspora in the Americas while the impact of the trade on Africa itself is generally ignored. Other dimensions of this problem on the African continent are: (i) the existence of a wide gap between published research works and their impact on school and university curricula; (ii) the treatment of the TTEA from the perspective of European expansion or the abolition campaign; and (iii) the treatment of the subject from a narrow perspective in the school curricula of the former colonial powers. These factors have provided students with a fragmented picture of the history of the trade and of Africa. The details of the organization of the trade are given greater emphasis than its impact on Africa and the African diaspora.

The collection of oral data is especially difficult as Africans in Africa are reluctant or unwilling to recall the trade and its bitter memory. Yet, explains Soumonni (2001), the oral traditions are vital to historical reconstruction where there is inadequate written documentation from within Africa. The inadequacy of written documents is used as another excuse to overlook the impact of the trade in Africa.

Ama Ata Aidoo (2001), Ghanaian writer and professor of literature, notes that even though Ghana played a major role in the trade and boasts most of the surviving forts and castles associated with it, she never heard anyone talk about the slave trade at home.

All traces of the trade seemed to have been erased from people's memories as soon as it was formally abolished. The events were either accidentally or deliberately silenced. Aidoo ventures to explain this silence as possibly the result of a collective amnesia resulting from pain and shame or a deliberate conspiracy of silence.

A deep sense of guilt and the African refusal to face up to its own responsibility in the TTEA is perceived by Mbembe (2001) as the explanation for the ambivalence around the conscious recall of slavery in Africa. He describes the silence in Africa as 'the silence of guilt' (p.26). Africans seek to erase the trail of brother murdering brother and for Membe, this results in an illusion that on both sides of the Atlantic, servitude and suffering were the same, which, he states, was not the case. He posits that, because of this, the traumatism and loss caused by the trade will always be different on both sides of the Atlantic. Consequently, Mbembe argues, appeals to race to provide a foundation for solidarity that is moral and political cannot hope to evoke a real response unless continental Africans have reconsidered the TTEA and other forms of slavery as both a catastrophe visited upon them as well as an outcome of a history to which they contributed in their role as partners and by their treatment of other Africans.

## Brazil

Brazil now has the second largest black population in the world, after Nigeria, some 113 years after the abolition of slavery in that country. The black population, classified as mulattos and blacks by the Instituto Brasiliero de Geografia e Estatística, is estimated at 70 million people. Yet, according to Dos Santos Gomes (2001) the experience of the black population in Brazil is one of invisibility and inequality despite their quantitative significance. During slavery, black Brazilians united their forces in the *quilombos* (communities of enslaved Africans who ran away) and it was the *quilombo* which, historically, gave birth to resistance against racism in Brazil.

However, Sansone (2001) states that there has been an exorcism of slavery out of the pantheon of black cultural production in Brazil. There has been no attempt to build a monument to slavery or a slavery museum in Rio and Salvador where there are very large concentrations of black Brazilians, and indeed the largest concentrations of people of African descent outside of Africa. Rather, the effort has been to exorcize the pain of slavery in these sites that have been important in the history of slavery in Brazil. Monuments erected in 1988 to observe the centenary of abolition highlighted those who fought against slavery; there was no interest in representing the embarrassing fact of slavery itself. Brazil has had a relatively short period without slavery. Not only are the scars of slavery still fresh, but one avoids solidifying memories into monuments as the legacies of slavery live on (Sansone in Oostindie, 2001).

In Brazil, as in many developing countries, heritage has not yet been made part of the political claims of civil society. Sansone states that, as there is no ethno-racial politics in Brazil, there is little room for the commemoration of past wrongs through a monument to slavery. It is only within religion that there is the consistent remembrance of slavery in Brazilian society. This is particularly so in the case of the Umbanda, the domain of the syncretism of Afro-Brazilian religions. The absence of discussion in Brazil about constructing a monument to slavery generates problems. While there have been signs of improvement, the official representations of the nation need increased symbolic inclusion of Afro-Brazilians. There is almost no public debate on this topic. Even though black Brazilians represent almost half of the population, there is still a relative absence of institutionalized negotiation and symbolic reparation for those who have suffered the most.

## *The United States of America*

The USA is said to be unique in devoting most attention to symbolic remorse in the latter part of the twentieth century. This symbolic remorse is reflected in a proliferation of museums, libraries and various types of monuments, all of which make use of non-formal educational intervention in the task of memorializing the history of the TTEA in the context of the USA. Since only an estimated five per cent of the enslaved Africans were taken to North America, Allison Blakely (2001), professor of European and comparative history in the USA, explains the flurry of activity in the USA as arising principally from two factors: (i) as a result of the North American tendency to emphasize colour over class, the continuation of the legacy of slavery was more pronounced in the USA than in those racially mixed societies, such as Brazil, where the lines connecting the descendants of enslaved Africans to their ancestry were deliberately blurred; and (ii) slavery and the TTEA were sharp contradictions to American ideals. The logic inherent in this was that the state would have to function within the ideals upon which it was based or lose its integrity and it is this second factor which Blakely presents as the single most important explanation for the attention in the USA to symbolic remorse.

All aspects of the trade and slavery are commemorated in the USA under the following general categories: the Middle Passage, the institution of American slavery, and liberation struggles as depicted by the Amistad mutiny, the Underground Railroad and the civil rights movement statutes. Monuments, museums and plantation re-enactments are also among the forms of commemoration. In more recent times, websites on the internet serve as reinforcements of these forms.

In the realm of academia, the legacy of slavery has been addressed through the establishment of college departments and scholarly black studies symposia; through the publication of innumerable books and articles and the mainstreaming of the concept of African diaspora. In the 1970s the rapid increase in the numbers of black studies programmes and departments peaked. However, since then, they have declined sharply. This has been a result of not receiving full institutional status and shrinking educational budgets.

Despite these efforts in the American context, Robinson (2000) asserts that too many blacks hate themselves and that ignorance of the history of Africa before slavery is one reason for black people's self-degradation. Robinson laments what he perceives as black people blaming and disparaging themselves but rarely those who are responsible for their situation today. This in itself is a potentially controversial position to adopt as there are those who would argue, including black people themselves, that blacks today must assume responsibility for whatever difficulties in life they encounter. Such a position tends to reveal an insufficient appreciation for the legacies of historical phenomena such as the transatlantic trade in enslaved Africans.

A consequence of the ignorance of Africa's long and distinguished history previous to slavery and of blacks as world innovators in the sciences and humanities is a pervasive global belief that blacks are inherently inferior. There is a crushing loss of confidence among blacks themselves. Robinson states that this gives rise to a downward spiral of self-hate, public black self-disparagement and anger.

Horton (2006) describes the subject of slavery in American history as 'an uncomfortable national dialogue'. While Americans see themselves as a people who love freedom, historical scholarship spanning the last two generations has revealed that national actions in the USA, are not always consistent with the declared American commitment to freedom. For Horton, it is this self-image of being a liberty loving people that induces in Americans feelings of embarrassment, guilt and disillusionment when considering the role of race and slavery in American history. Attempts to locate these characteristics of American history in American memory are likely to incur defensiveness, anger and confrontation. At the same time, such responses reveal the importance of history for Americans as it is linked to national and personal identity. Horton identifies an American tendency to turn a blind eye to history that does not reflect well on the nation and that causes discomfort. He notes that one cannot ignore the past and must learn from it, even when it provokes shame and pain.

American national demographics indicate that racial and cultural minorities are rapidly defining American society. In such a society, history education, with the purpose of cross-cultural understanding, should be embraced as an important means of achieving social stability and coexistence. This cannot be a task assigned only to the formal education system and such education in public spaces must also be accorded priority. In both formal and non-formal education, the sensitivity and difficulty of treating with the role of slavery is a challenge to be confronted. This is a challenge which the USA shares with all multicultural societies, and especially those of the African diaspora.

Descendants of enslaved Africans in the Caribbean, North America and Europe share a common past, marked by the transatlantic trade in enslaved Africans, with the descendants of those who were the financial benefactors of the trade and the slavery system in the Caribbean. This past will continue to elicit denial, guilt, shame and ambivalence.

Mbembe (2001) identifies as the source of ambivalence surrounding the recall of slavery the deliberate repression of slavery memories by the descendants of enslaved Africans in some parts of the New World. There is a denial of the tragedy explaining their existence in the present. This denial is reflective of a refusal to acknowledge ancestral origins and to think of a phenomenon in history around which feelings of shame linger. The result of this is the failure to attribute importance to regaining contact with oneself and one's origins.

## TRAUMA AND INSTITUTIONALIZED RACISM – THE AFRICAN AMERICAN SITUATION

Blacks consequently are considerably overrepresented among the desperately poor in America. Robinson (2000) describes African Americans as having been largely overwhelmed by a majority culture that wronged them, emptied their memories, undermined their self-esteem and stripped away their self-definition.

Joy DeGruy Leary (2002), African American psychologist, addresses the manifestations of what she terms Post Traumatic Slave Syndrome among people of African ancestry in the United States. She identifies a lack of a sense of self or a 'vacant esteem' as one of the most important problems facing people of African heritage in the USA today. This she attributes to a failure of American society to confront history and reverse its wrongs. In her doctoral dissertation on African American male youth violence entitled 'Trying to kill the part of you that isn't loved' DeGruy Leary (2001) asserts that the American slavery experience was founded exclusively on the concept of the racial inferiority of Africans. While acknowledging the difficulty of establishing a direct relationship between African Americans' experience of slavery and the major social phenomenon in the USA of African American male youth violence, she nonetheless points to research conducted on other ethnic groups with an experience of oppression and trauma, as presented in the work of American psychologist Yael Danieli (1998), for example, which puts forward the trauma-transcendence legacy model and provides evidence that:

> survivor syndromes exist and are pervasive in the human development of second and third generation offspring. The characteristics of the survivor syndrome include: stress, self-doubt, problems with aggression and a number of psychological and interpersonal relationship problems with family members and others. (DeGruy Leary, 2001, p.9)

DeGruy Leary's dissertation sought to determine whether issues of respect and racial socialization were related to the use of violence among African American male youths. The findings of the study included hypersensitivity of incarcerated African American youth, a characteristic noted among trauma survivors and reported by Danieli (1998) in the *International Handbook of Multigenerational Legacies of Trauma*. The dissertation reports the likely impact upon black American youth of feeling disrespected. DeGruy Leary found that incarcerated youths in her study felt disrespected by the typical representatives of socializing institutions and by others in their social circle. She found further that these youths may not be able to ignore personal feelings of disrespect or criticism as a result of their frustration and anger over not being valued by others.

These findings resonate in the writing of Robinson (2000) who observes that, having been treated so badly for so long, African Americans are angrier than many would think. Though citizens with full rights, African Americans have defected emotionally from a society whose white majority ensured for blacks the death of any sense of cultural ownership.

William Cross (1998), African American psychologist, does not embrace the application of the trauma-transcendence legacy model to American enslavement of blacks. He reasons that while trauma conveys ideas of an event that is sudden and unpredictable, slavery as an institution lasted nearly 400 years. Trauma is associated with victims, pain and damage; slavery was a multidimensional, long-term experience in which there was both black victimization and 'effective black coping'. Cross acknowledges that the episodes of oppression which followed American slavery and still exist do have the potential for trauma. However, he argues that contemporary black problems have their source in contemporary circumstances rather than in dysfunctional attitudes arising out of the slavery experience and existing in the present as 'a legacy of the trauma of slavery' (p.387). In support of this position he postulates that formerly enslaved Africans had higher achievement motivation; eagerly supported their children's education; were centred on family values and aimed to become a pivotal group in the economy and culture of America. He attributes contemporary negative black birthing and marriage patterns to institutionalized racism, workplace discrimination and reduced employment opportunities, and points to white racism and not 'black deficits' as the real legacy of slavery.

Beverly Daniel Tatum (1992) states that slavery and its social, psychological and economic legacies have shaped forever black-white race relations in the USA. She explains that, in that country, cultural racism consisting of cultural images and messages communicating an ideology of white superiority and the inferiority of people of colour are pervasive. The media, ethnic jokes, lack of information about the achievements of oppressed groups all convey negativity which breeds prejudice (arising out of stereotypes, omissions, distortions and usually a result of inadequate information). A member of a group that is stereotyped may even, to some degree, internalize the stereotyped categories of his or her group — a phenomenon which occurs often and is referred to as internalized oppression. She advances the view that while one may not be responsible for prejudice and racism, there is a collective responsibility for its eradication, a responsibility that is not relieved with declarations that one is not at fault.

Limiting an understanding of racism to prejudice does not explain sufficiently the continuing existence of racism. Tatum (1992) uses Wellman's (1977) definition of racism as a system of advantage that has race as its basis. It therefore goes beyond personal mindsets determined by racial prejudice and involves cultural messages, institutional policies and practices and the beliefs and actions of individuals. In the USA, the system favours whites and works to the disadvantage of people of colour. Antiracist educators and consultants also define racism as 'prejudice plus power'. The combination of racial prejudice and social power, with access to social, cultural and economic resources and decision-making, results in institutionalized racist policies and practices. There is also passive racism, for example, the omission of people of colour from the school curriculum and failure to deal with difficult race-related issues. According to Tatum, racism in America is so institutionalized as to be the status quo. Failure to acknowledge the existence of the system of advantage perpetuates it. People of colour are adversely impacted by racism. For many whites gaining a new awareness of the benefits of white privilege in a racist system awakens significant pain along with feelings of anger and guilt; emotions which are uncomfortable and can forestall further discussion. Understanding that racism is a contradiction of justice destroys their belief in a just world. Tatum asserts further that both black and white adults are hesitant about speaking to children about racism, out of fear that they can stir up problems where none existed before.

## Students' psychological responses to race-related content

Race related memories have emotions attached to them. Recognition of this can facilitate insights regarding the management of students' responses to the subject of the TTEA in the classroom setting. According to Tatum, these responses can include anger, confusion, surprise, sadness, and embarrassment.

Students often do not want to admit to the reality of racism, and usually they deal with the unease of learning about racism by going into denial, explains Tatum. When they acquire a better understanding of the impact of racism on their lives, students on the receiving end of racism often feel pain and anger. White students, with an increased understanding of racism, experience painful feelings of guilt.

Avoidance of the subject of racism serves as one means for students to escape uncomfortable feelings. Because they are affected by racism, students of colour do not focus on their own prejudices but generally want to know why racism exists and how it affects them. Tatum indicates that with increased understanding of racism in the USA, students then begin to notice its legacy within themselves. White students reflect on their own thinking and behaviour influenced by racial stereotypes and students of colour usually identify their own internalized negative attitudes about their own racial group or other racial groups.

The subject of slavery serves as one of the limited ways in which the school curriculum incorporates the black experience and young African American students feel embarrassed when it is discussed. Their discomfort arises from the portrayal of blacks as helpless victims as there are rarely classroom discussions focusing on the acts of rebellion and resistance on the part of the enslaved Africans (Tatum, 1999). White teachers have communicated the discomfort they too sometimes feel with the subject of slavery and the pain of the history of race relations in the USA. Tatum states that something is wrong with the approach used if there are such feelings of discomfort. While not negating the need to treat with past and present racism honestly, she points to the necessity of empowering children and adults with the vision that change is possible, and in this regard proposes Cross's (1991) Model of Black Identity Development as a strategy to address issues relating to identity formation among black students. The model assumes that it is important for one's psychological health to feel good about being a member of one's group, without this being based on notions or feelings of superiority. It establishes five stages in the process of identity development. These processes contribute to an appreciation of the ways in which knowledge can help to shape identity.

## Black people's identity and self-esteem

*Identity* is significantly influenced by the messages communicated by the world around; omission from cultural images also impacts upon identity. In the context of the USA, subordinate groups function within parameters set by dominant groups. Power and authority are held by the dominant group which determines the ways in which those should be acceptably used. This includes determining whose history schools will teach and the relationships which society will validate.

To the extent that the targeted group internalizes the images that the dominant group projects to its members, they may find it difficult to believe in their own ability. Culture is saturated with the dominant worldview so that everyone will learn it, and information about those subordinated by the dominant group is usually stereotypical. Unequal relationships hold risks and consequently members of the subordinated group covertly resist or undermine the power of the dominant group. This is reflected in popular culture in which jokes, stories and folk tales (for example, Anansi stories) recount the outwitting of the more powerful by the subordinate.

Nicéphore Soglo (2001), President of the Republic of Benin, 1991-1996, laments black people's internalization of the racist message of their inferiority; that whatever the beginnings and the paths of the slave trade, the results were the same: self-contempt and a tragic internalized sense of inferiority.

Oguibe (2001) writing about slavery and the diaspora imagination expresses the view that the souls of the descendants of enslaved Africans carry a void from being brutally severed from their place of origin and by time. The search for identity forms part of the legacy of the TTEA for the descendants of enslaved Africans. He describes slavery as a recurrent theme in the imagination of the diaspora it has spawned because while a wound may heal, a scar does not fade. Oguibe even doubts the prospects for the healing of the deep wounds of slavery. For the sake of guarding against its repetition, he advocates keeping its memory alive so that both victim and perpetrator may 'live in the shadow of its knowledge.' (Oguibe in Oostindie 2001, p.100).

## The English-speaking Caribbean

Goulbourne (2001) notes that, in the Caribbean, the legacies of slavery still have to be confronted at the levels of society and the state. While poets, novelists, academics, and painters, for example, have all addressed the slavery past, there remains a need to confront squarely what this means for ' present patterns of ownership, social integration and control of social, economic and political power...in terms of policy and public discussion' (p.129).

According to Hilary McD. Beckles (2001), Caribbean society continues to display the legacies of African slavery in western modernity. Richard Goodridge (1998), Caribbean historian, identifies as a central issue in the teaching of African history in Barbados, the need to also address issues of low self-esteem of a black population that has been oppressed for centuries. In the early 1990s in Barbados, instilling some knowledge of Africa was part of an effort to build self-esteem and confidence to counter a deep, insidious inferiority complex among the greater part of the student population, particularly among the males. Goodridge (1998) argues that African history should not be taught merely to glorify or praise, but should be presented as representing part of the process of human development to which Africa clearly contributed. It was also thought to be necessary to help and encourage the children, through this effort, to be vibrant and creative and to develop character and identity. These concerns would seem to point to a belief that history should play a role in nation building.

In other parts of the English-speaking Caribbean, there is also the perception of a weak African Caribbean identity thought to be the result of a lack of respect for people of dark skin, especially in multi-ethnic societies. As in the USA the experience of being disrespected can undermine Afro-Caribbean people's sense of self and of having a rightful place in society. In such societies, dark-skinned people of Indian ancestry are also perceived to suffer similarly. Some believe that if this issue is not dealt with as seriously as are issues of the economy, the minds of people of African descent will continue to be enslaved in the twenty-first century. African-Caribbean self-disparagement may be reflected in practices of skin bleaching and a conformance to white standards of beauty — all taken as evidence that 'Black is not seen as beautiful and that Black people have internalized the myth of Black inferiority and white superiority' (Verene Shepherd, in Hall and Benn (eds.) 2000, p.54). Unlike Cross (1998) in the context of the USA, Shepherd, Caribbean historian, advances the 'legacy of slavery model' as an explanation for a number of social phenomena in the English-speaking Caribbean, including the system of education having a negative impact on African-Caribbean identity. It appears, therefore, that despite emancipation and development agendas that have led to many achievements, including great strides in civil society on the part of Caribbean people of African descent, the issues of identity, pride in one's heritage and self-acceptance remain serious challenges.

Lloyd Best, Caribbean intellectual, activist and Trinidad and Tobago newspaper columnist, in an article headlined 'The Afro-Saxon Heritage' in the *Express Newspaper* of June 14, 2003 shies away from arguing the case of an African-Caribbean identity crisis. Rather, he states that all strata of society experience the same dominant psychology of dispossession and struggle, wherever they may come from and even after five decades of self-government. He recognizes a need to examine the features of Caribbean civilization as a whole to understand where it has reached and the facts which have contributed to it being where it is. Such an examination he views as being indispensable, if only for the reason of the diabolical dynamics of the legacies of the history of enslavement.

In Trinidad and Tobago, as a possible solution to addressing issues perceived as relating to identity among Trinidad and Tobago youth of African heritage, calls have been made for a more central place to be accorded African ancestry and heritage as an element in fostering a greater sense of self-worth. While such arguments generate much debate within the multicultural context of Trinidad and Tobago society, they reflect the degree of concern about the social ills which seem to plague black youths, and particularly black male youths in Trinidad and Tobago. Education is held up as a critical component in the process of self-realization and social stability and it is, therefore, appropriate to examine the contribution of the education system to addressing this issue.

Patricia Mohammed (2004), Caribbean scholar and activist in the fields of Gender Studies and Caribbean iconography, cites the doctoral dissertation of Emmanuel Kwaku Senah, a Ghanaian living in Trinidad and Tobago, who recounts questions posed to him by children in Trinidad and Tobago during his visits to schools. These questions revealed the children's desire to know what Africans today did with their slaves; whether he was a slave; and why black people sold their own people into slavery. Mohammed wonders why younger generations are left with such notions of their past and how they feel about themselves. Her conclusions support the perception of the existence of an Afro-Caribbean crisis of identity and self-esteem. Mohammed states:

A "burden of blackness", slavery and African society appear synonymous in their vocabulary of understanding, and make for an unhealthy stream of consciousness with which to construct a confident present and future…If the search for one's roots is also pride in ethnicity, then we need to dispel some myths while we create new ones and more liberating truths that may emerge in the process (p.6).

Mohammed suggests that there has been inadequate transparency and accessibility of the study of Africa and slavery to most people of African descent and that further, such study should not be limited to African descended peoples, just as people of all ethnic groups should also have access to studies of East Indians, Chinese and Jews.

Eintou Springer, cultural activist and poet laureate of Port of Spain, Trinidad and Tobago encourages the celebration of the African but notes that this requires that the African be aware that she or he has something to celebrate and that this can only be done by imparting the kind of knowledge that empowers.

Shepherd (2000) suggests that the transmission of African ancestors' positive stories and legacies related to survival and seeking to live lives characterized by decency and dignity could serve as a source of empowerment. She calls for public speakers on the theme of emancipation to become familiar with the revisionist works on slavery and to read comparative material as opposed to relying only on traditional texts. The revisionists focus to a greater extent on people's agency, while not negating the brutality of slavery.

Revisiting the actions of the enslaved peoples, as opposed to focusing exclusively on the perpetuation of colonialist mentalities, draws attention to the Africans' resistance to being captured in Africa, their resistance to being shipped across the Middle Passage, and their resistance to enslavement in the Caribbean — perspectives which are not usually included in public discussions on slavery. These perspectives emphasize the positive attitudes, values and behaviours of the enslaved Africans in relation to, inter alia, family, sexuality, economic autonomy and masculinity, areas of the lives of people of African ancestry often targeted with negative comment and interpretations. Knowledge of Africans' resistance to their enslavement and of the principles and values that were important to them can help to shape the identity of students of African descent, since an outcome could be a deeper understanding of their history that promotes feeling good about being a member of their group, thus contributing to their psychological health.

Springer, in Trinidad and Tobago, provides some direction in her recommendation to expose Caribbean youths and especially those of African heritage to Caribbean writers such as Walter Rodney, Eric Williams, George Lamming and Earl Lovelace who put the African protagonist on the page. She recognizes the function of literature as one of liberating the mind, giving cultural confidence and providing the social history absent from the curriculum.

Caribbean scholars such as Shepherd and public commentators such as Springer, identify the need for ministries of education and culture to review the content of textbooks for the removal of stereotypic and racist representations of people of African origin; for the production of textbooks which make research findings accessible to secondary school students and to the masses, and for the development of educational programmes on African and Caribbean history to ensure a full understanding of their historical legacy. Shepherd (2000) argues that such programmes should be made mandatory for students at the secondary and tertiary levels of education. A similar position is adopted by Koïchiro Matsuura (2004), Director General of UNESCO, who considers education about the TTEA a priority and calls for it to have a mandatory place in education worldwide. Matsuura states:

> As a matter of urgency this major episode in the history of humanity, whose consequences are permanently imprinted in the world's geography and economy, should take its full place in the school textbooks and curricula of every country in the world. (p.42)

Such a proclamation on the part of the head of the leading United Nations agency for education sends a clear signal of the importance of teaching the TTEA.

## THE HAITIAN REVOLUTION AND ITS INFLUENCE IN THE CARIBBEAN AND THE AMERICAS

The Haitian Revolution was the first major manifestation in the Caribbean of thought similar to that of the Age of Enlightenment in Western Europe. Oruno D. Lara (2004), French West Indian historian based in Paris, in discussing the influence of the Haitian Revolution in the Caribbean and the Americas noted that the rebellion of the enslaved Africans in Santo Domingo in August 1791 ignited a general insurrection which led to the abolition of slavery and to the unilateral declaration of independence in Haiti. It was the commencement of a process of the dismantling of the colonial system of which the TTEA was a critical component. The Haitian Revolution sparked in the Americas a liberation movement which combined the ideas of freedom and equality and paved the way to independence. According to Lara (2004), from 1795 to 1848 Haitians were involved in the liberation process in the Caribbean and the Americas. They engaged in freeing cargoes of enslaved Africans carried in Portuguese, Spanish and Cuban vessels; in undermining Spanish possessions; in the gradual destruction of the proslavery system in Guadeloupe and Martinique; in rebellions of enslaved Africans in British Guyana, Jamaica, Puerto Rico and in the USA, particularly in Louisiana.

Haiti also rendered assistance to Francisco de Miranda in Venezuela in February 1806, and to Simon Bolivar in 1815 and 1816. In 1816 and 1820, the Haitian government agreed to provide weapons and ammunition to the leaders of the independent movements in Mexico and Colombia respectively, on the condition that slavery would be abolished in these countries. Lara indicates that after the abolition of slavery in the French colonies in 1848 the Haitian Revolution was adopted as the model for advocacy of the independence of Guadeloupe.

The experience of the Haitian Revolution and its impact throughout the Caribbean and the Americas, therefore, is indicative of the impact of the TTEA on its victims and the fervour with which they sought and did pursue freedom, emancipation and justice for themselves and for others.

Hector and Casimir (2004) reviewing what they refer to as 'Haiti's long XIX Century' begin with the proclamation of independence of

Haiti on January 1, 1804, as the critical, enduring, contested moment. This moment gave birth to a nation and people which the world at the time had not imagined possible. The successful revolt of the enslaved Africans in Haiti in 1791 resulted in both personal freedom for some 500,000, and the achievement of citizenship and nationhood. In order to secure its patrimony, the Haitian state sought unceasingly to negotiate with imperial nations whose principles and practice threatened its sovereignty. Haiti's endurance in maintaining its independence became a source of embarrassment to such imperial states that continued to believe in the efficacy of socioeconomic systems based on the principle of white over black. Hector and Casimir underscore the extent to which the Haitian state evolved with an ideological and realpolitik context of fear of internal subversion and external defeat, conditions that distorted and derailed the original project of regional and global black redemption. While the urban and rural masses in Haiti were demanding their rights, the great powers in the international community saw it as their responsibility to belittle the Haitian elites and to discriminate against them openly. Haiti's long nineteenth century was characterized by alternating periods of real progress and definite decline in its uncompromising pursuit of national development but which today has imploded.

The image contamination of Haiti to which students and even their teachers are exposed stands as a legacy still subverting Haiti's quest for freedom. Haiti, in the aftermath of the Haitian Revolution, continues to be denigrated rather than celebrated and persistently discriminated against in the international community. Calls for Caribbean people to embrace Haiti and her past can only succeed in the future through quality education about the Haitian Revolution and its cultural aftershocks being made available to Caribbean youths.

Beckles (2001) indicates that Toussaint L'Ouverture is symbolic of the vision on which the hopes and ideals of Caribbean citizens were focused and which set them on the path to citizenship and nation building. The ideological rhetoric of emancipation was the context for attaining citizenship. Popular radicalism was expressed through the concept 'massa day done' (Beckles, 2001, p.92). This was an invocation of people's views about slavery, born of memory and pain, and around which Eric Williams built his career. It situated him within the tradition of radical anti-slavery leaders.

The end of Empire and the creation of national independence were brought about by the quest for social justice through citizenship. The struggle against slavery and the victory of emancipation saw nation states emerging from plantations. Enslaved blacks emerged as leaders of democratic nation states, thus constituting a revolutionary development in modernity. The heroes and heroines of the fight against slavery and its structures in the post-emancipation period were honoured by the new nations.

According to Beckles (2001) Jamaica and Barbados stand as examples of national independence being accompanied by celebration of national heroes and heroines, persons who challenged the colonial order. Nanny, leader of a Maroon clan in Jamaica who engaged in a protracted war against British troops; Sam Sharpe, who led the revolution of the enslaved Africans in January 1831; the peasant leader, Paul Bogle and William Gordon, who in the 1865 rebellion inspired the struggle for black land ownership, have all been enshrined in the Jamaican pantheon of heroes and heroines.

Barbados, in 1998, followed the example of Jamaica with the official recognition of its national heroes and the declaration of August 1 as a national holiday. Bussa, Sarah Gill and Samuel Prescod, the first three Barbadian national icons fought for freedom during slavery. Antislavery revolutionary leaders fighting for civil rights and visionaries of national independence have also been recognized in Guyana, Grenada, Dominica and St. Vincent and the Grenadines

Notwithstanding the pervasiveness of the ideology 'massa day done' and the successes of the independence movements, colonial relationships continue to entrap some people in the Caribbean and black economic marginalization continues to be a reality.

Caribbean societies are presented as 'monuments to freedom and incubators of liberationist political philosophies' (Beckles in Oostindie 2001, p.90), which made it possible for free and enslaved working people to bring to life the vision of enlightenment through 'emancipation in action' (Beckles, in Oostindie 2001, p.90).

The struggle of blacks for freedom was prolonged and marked by their commitment to social idealism. Blacks offered the most radical voice in the emancipation discourse and their voices continue to shape politics and identity in the Caribbean. While Caribbean society is representative of a people who have emerged from great despair and bondage and in which African ethnic, cultural and spiritual survival must be celebrated, Beckles (2001) says that the process of emergence 'is perilously incomplete' (p.90). Indeed, several writers point to the issues of black people's self-esteem and identity as evidence of the problems associated with the process of emergence.

## THE ISSUE OF HUMAN DEVELOPMENT

The process of people becoming capital under the conditions of the TTEA affected their development, but human development was a key component of Enlightenment thought. Key concepts of 'Enlightenment' thought included the following: (i) human experience is the basis of human understanding of truth, and authority is not to be preferred over experience; (ii) human history is largely one of progress; and (iii) human beings can be improved through education and the development of their rational facilities (Richard Hooker, 1996). These espoused principles of Enlightenment thought were betrayed with the organization and conduct of the TTEA, particularly as for the enslaved Africans in the Caribbean, unlike the situation with the Amerinidans and indentured labourers from India, there was no mitigation of the impact of slavery or system of protection and care designed to ameliorate their condition.

Human beings endeavour to improve opportunities for those persons they define as human and to do this they are driven to provide what is necessary (for example, things and opportunities) to assist people in their development. Meaningful human activity leads to people being made productive and more human. Work that is alienating and dehumanizing does not promote human development. People must have a deep sense of the favourable difference they make in the world if they are to be empowered and if the enterprise of human development is to be sustained.

Far from developing human beings as embodied in Enlightenment thought, the TTEA undermined human life, thus securing its place as a phenomenon in world history. While whites involved in the TTEA argued that they were advancing the Africans, their victims, the enslaved Africans, saw the TTEA as the means of their destruction.

Chapter 2

# Background And Conceptual Framework

## The UNESCO Slave Route Project

In 1997 the General Conference of UNESCO launched an international project on the 'Slave Route' and in so doing provided an international framework for multidisciplinary reflection on the underlying causes, mechanisms and consequences of the trade in enslaved Africans. The Director General of UNESCO, Federico Mayor, in presenting the justification for the Slave Route Project, stated that the very fact of ignoring or deliberately obscuring major historical events can, in itself, constitute an obstacle to peace. He identified the objective of the Slave Route Project as the spread of awareness and more detailed knowledge of the various aspects of the TTEA (Transatlantic Trade in Enslaved Africans) to enable the people directly involved, as well as the public at large, to come to terms with this shared memory, and thus responsibly breathe new life into cooperation among them.

It is within the context of UNESCO's Slave Route Project that the organization launched the UNESCO Associated Schools Project Network (ASPNet) Transatlantic Slave Trade Education Project in Haiti in August 1998 to coincide with the first international observance, on 23 August, of the International Day to Commemorate the Abolition of the Slave Trade. This launch, the first meeting of an international task force, assembled eminent scholars on the subject of the TTEA from the Americas/Caribbean, Africa and Europe. The mandate of the task force was to advise UNESCO on the implementation of the project, to produce relevant materials and to support the schools and teachers participating in the project.

## The UNESCO Associated Schools Project Network (ASPnet) "Transatlantic Slave Trade (TST) Education Project"

The rationale for the ASPnet TST Education Project, agreed upon by members of the international task force, focused on the threat of the loss of knowledge of the TTEA as the lessons of this tragedy may be forgotten over time thereby reducing sensitivity to this episode of inhumanity. This threat is amplified by the omission or lack of attention paid to the TTEA in classroom teaching at the secondary school level. Study of the TTEA in secondary schools throughout the Atlantic world and beyond can help protect this knowledge and highlight its importance as an essential part of the collective human heritage.

The rationale articulated for the Project is also located within the extraordinary scale of the TTEA, the depth of human suffering it engendered and the considerable cultural, economic and technological contributions made by enslaved Africans and their descendants to the modern Atlantic world. This unique historical phenomenon is recognized by UNESCO as providing a critical element in the global framework within which the 1948 Universal Declaration of Human Rights was conceived and propagated.

### Objectives of the ASPnet TST Education Project

The report of the first meeting of the task force for the ASPnet TST Education Project held in Port au Prince, Haiti in August 1998 identified the following Project objectives:

- To increase knowledge about the slave trade as a human tragedy, study its various intercultural dimensions (transfer of culture, knowledge, science and technology) and demonstrate its overall impact in shaping the Atlantic world.
- To inculcate desired attitudinal values among students in relation to citizenship, cooperation, human rights and responsibilities, democracy and freedom.
- To provide opportunities for exchanges among teachers and students in support of the creation of a network promoting

educational activity to generate knowledge about the slave trade.
- To facilitate teacher training to improve pedagogical approaches about the slave trade.
- To develop and produce appropriate texts and multimedia educational materials to provide adequate institutional support for teaching about the slave trade and to respond to the need for healing of psychological wounds.

Four main educational approaches were identified for use in the Project: (i) in-school education; (ii) extra-curricular activities; (iii) distance education; and (iv) cooperation between higher education and secondary school education. The task force members determined that introducing and reinforcing teaching about the TTEA would require both cognitive and affective approaches, with emphasis on intercultural learning. From 1998 to 2005 the ASPnet Project was funded by the Norwegian Agency for Development (NORAD).

The discussion of process issues and challenges of the pedagogy of the historiography of the TTEA focuses on some major thematic areas. It is intended that the consideration of these issues will serve as a contribution that can inform teacher education curricula for enhancing teachers' pedagogical content knowledge of the TTEA, its causes, consequences and legacies.

This study was informed, in part, by two surveys undertaken within the context of the Project. Specifically these surveys are: (i) a survey of students' knowledge and attitudes relating to the TTEA conducted in 2000 and (ii) an evaluation of the UNESCO Associated Schools 'Transatlantic Slave Trade Education Project' conducted in 2002.

## UNESCO Associated Schools 'Transatlantic Slave Trade Education Project': Survey of Knowledge and Attitudes on the Transatlantic Trade in Enslaved Africans

In his report on responses of students who participated in a UNESCO survey of students' knowledge and attitudes on the TTEA undertaken at the inception of the Project, Hilary Beckles (2000) indicated that the objective of the survey instrument was to gather information on broad knowledge tendencies and patterns and to arrive at a general understanding of attitudinal types and their sources. Consequently, it was not seen as necessary to utilize advanced scientific sampling methodologies.

The survey targeted students aged 14 to 16 and was designed to capture the following:

> general knowledge of the TTEA; attitudes and opinions held about the TTEA, its legacies and related public discourses; sources of knowledge, attitudes and opinions

Beckles (2000) also pointed out in his report that the selection of the questions regarding knowledge was guided by a concept of knowledge that students could reasonably be expected to have, based on information that was generally available to the public through mass media and school syllabi in the academic areas of national and world history. The questionnaire was not intended as a means of determining students' historical knowledge for the purpose of intelligence assessment. Rather, its purpose was to gather information on the nature of teaching and the state of curriculum development with respect to the TTEA.

## Structure of enquiry

The knowledge component of the questionnaire was formulated using two multiple-choice formats: (i) ten statements solicited a response within three categories: true, false, don't know; and (ii) twenty questions solicited the correct response from four statements, including a 'don't know' category.

A Likert Scale was used to solicit attitudes and opinions with five possible responses: agree, strongly agree, disagree, strongly disagree, and no opinion. In relation to sources of knowledge and opinions students were asked to rank eleven possible sources by order of importance. These were: family discussion, television, radio, cinema, books/magazines, public discussion, internet, newspapers, audio-visual aids, museums and teachers. Four categories were provided for students to locate the importance of each source: very much, somewhat, very little and none.

## *Summary of quantitative overview of the survey*

Twenty countries and 90 schools participated in the survey, with a total of 2,075 responses with a fairly even level of participation across schools. The highest level of participation in the survey was found in the Americas (46.15 per cent) and most of these schools came from the Caribbean – 37 out of 42 schools. Europe accounted for 28.5 per cent of the total number of participating schools and Africa 25.28 per cent.

## *Significant observations*

Beckles' (2000) analysis of the results of the survey resulted in ten significant observations, seven of which are presented as follows:

1. Scientific knowledge held by students about the TTEA was underdeveloped across the regions. Responses indicated that the majority of students in all regions did not possess sufficient knowledge to answer correctly more than 50 per cent of most questions. Less than 15 per cent of the 30 multiple-choice questions were answered correctly by more than 50 per cent of all students.
2. The lowest performance level was recorded by European students, an indication of the inadequate teaching priority attached to this subject in school, and the significant degree of inaccessibility to scientific knowledge.
3. There were significant differences in students' performances when knowledge was assessed on a national basis. Results indicated that teaching the TTEA was effectively restricted to narrow nationalist considerations and known imperial boundaries; students were not encouraged to conceive of the TTEA as an issue that transcends domestic/imperial political questions and geographical boundaries.

## Sample questions

### Goree Island/cowrie shells

The majority of African students demonstrated knowledge of Gorée Island and the use of cowrie shells while very few students from the Americas and Europe did. The majority of students from all regions, however, knew what was meant by the term 'Middle Passage'.

### Victor Schoelcher/William Wilberforce

Most students from Benin, a former French colony, recognized Schoelcher, the French abolitionist, but few recognized Wilberforce, the English abolitionist. The reverse was true with respect to Ghana, a former English colony where Wilberforce was generally recognized but Schoelcher was not. In Cuba and Brazil, former Spanish and Portuguese colonies respectively, neither the English nor French abolitionist was recognized by a significant number of students.

4. Despite the low levels of knowledge across regions, most students expressed attitudes and opinions indicating sensitivity to the tragic nature and harmful consequences of the TTEA.
5. African students were not the most knowledgeable, though their countries carry the evidence of the most visible, living memories.
6. Caribbean students, particularly those from the Anglophone region, seemed most informed; the regional curriculum review workshops indicated that in these Caribbean schools significant academic and socio-political attention was given to the study of the trade, slavery and their legacies where students studied history. At the other end of the scale was the European experience where curriculum development was least advanced and knowledge content with respect to the TTEA therefore most underdeveloped.
7. Teachers represented the primary source of knowledge of the TTEA for most students; teaching methods and materials, however, remained traditional rather than multi-disciplinary

and multimedia. Two important contrary trends were identified: (i) for Ghana, books and magazines featured more prominently than teachers; also, museum exhibitions closely rivalled teachers who occupied second place; with respect to Jamaica the role of television featured more prominently than teachers; (ii) for Spain and Portugal, the role of television, books and magazines closely approximated the importance attached to teachers.

In his summary of the findings of the survey, Beckles (2000) noted the following:

- Students' knowledge of the TTEA seemed to reflect observations made during the UNESCO Associated Schools' regional curriculum review workshops that only in the Anglophone Caribbean was there an attempt to teach the subject in a coherent and scientific fashion. But even so, the knowledge content of students seemed inadequate and insufficient in relation to the historical and social importance of the subject.
- The large number of 'don't know' responses indicated the extent of the lack of exposure to information, which was particularly significant given that the majority of students relied heavily upon the classroom to secure most of the knowledge they possess.
- There was considerable similarity between countries and regions with respect to attitudes and opinions about the TTEA and its legacies. While African students felt strongest about the negative impact of the trade upon the continent, and the question of securing compensation, students in Europe showed significant recognition of the trade as the most tragic development in modern history.
- The relative insignificance of multimedia, particularly the print and electronic press, was particularly illuminating and spoke probably to the continuing prevalence of traditional teaching and learning methods within schools across the regions.

## Findings of the Project Evaluation

Roger Levy of the University of Hertfordshire undertook an evaluation of the 'Transatlantic Slave Trade' Education Project on UNESCO's behalf in 2002. The findings were presented to the International Workshop for National Co-ordinators of the Project in Havana Cuba, between April 16 and 19, 2002 and to the Project's Fourth International Task Force Meeting held in Havana Cuba, April 20 and 21, 2002.

On the basis of the evaluation Levy established the following:

1. There was a continuing agenda to be addressed in teaching the TTEA and learning about the subject.
2. Such an agenda must include addressing learners' ignorance about Africa and especially Africa's history before and after the TTEA.
3. The value of cultural events as opportunities for teaching and learning the history of the TTEA.
4. The need to give priority to support for increasing teachers' knowledge of the TTEA, notably the dimensions of African history and of contemporary developments.

Levy also made some observations about the value of the Project and the desirability of its continuation based on the findings of the Project evaluation. He found that:

(i) the UNESCO Project made a significant impact upon teachers' knowledge of the TTEA, particularly their knowledge of events and experiences set in the country in which the teachers work. As the vast majority of pupils reported that teachers were their main source of knowledge, the Project strategy of seeking to increase the level of teachers' knowledge of the trade was justified;

(ii) the impact of the Project was particularly notable in those areas of the curriculum which relate to the experiences of enslaved Africans, the abolition of slavery, and continuing human rights issues;

(iii) learners' attitudes have been affected to a considerable extent by the Project;
(iv) Cultural events, such as Youth Encounters, have had a significant, even inspirational, effect on those who participated in them;
(v) the accessibility of resources has been a key factor in relation to use by both teachers and learners. The availability of accessible resources was associated with the Project having greater impact upon both teachers and learners;
(vi) participants at cultural events such as Youth Encounters have had access to unique resources and experiences which would not otherwise have been available to them;
(vii) the Project had less impact on teachers' and learners' knowledge and attitudes when the resources of curriculum time and teaching materials were relatively limited (notably concerning the history of Africa before the slave trade, and its effect upon Africa and on Latin America and the Caribbean);

The findings of both the knowledge and attitude survey and Project evaluation provide a good understanding of the status of teaching and learning the TTEA in selected countries in Africa, the Americas/Caribbean and Europe. In particular, both sets of findings underscore the fact that teachers are learners' main source of knowledge about the subject. This book attempts a closer examination of factors which confront teachers in the pedagogy of the TTEA.

## Conceptual Framework

The conceptual framework for the discussion rests on four pillars of which Lee Shulman's (1987) concept of pedagogical content knowledge is the most important. The other three pillars of this conceptual framework are: Jerry Rosiek's (2003) and Nate McCaughtry's (2004) work relating to the emotional dimension of pedagogical content knowledge; Lorrie Shepard's (2000) reformed vision of the curriculum; and concepts which pertain to human development. This conceptual framework informs the general discussion of issues and challenges in the pedagogy of the TTEA.

## PEDAGOGICAL CONTENT KNOWLEDGE

Pedagogical content knowledge is defined as 'that special amalgam of content and pedagogy that is uniquely the province of teachers, their own special form of professional understanding' (Shulman, 1987, p.7). The skills in conveying knowledge to others form part of being an expert teacher and these skills are referred to by Shulman as 'pedagogical content knowledge':

> it includes knowledge of the most effective examples, analogies, and explanations for key topics to a domain. It includes "the ways of representing and formulating the subject that makes it comprehensible to others" (Shulman 1986, p.9).

Though subject-matter experts, teachers must still be able to see their subject the way novices do. Pedagogical content knowledge is considered to be central to the knowledge base of the teaching profession and as being necessary for expert teaching. Aspects of pedagogical reasoning which are seen as explaining teacher cognition and behaviour are comprehension, transformation, instruction, evaluation, reflection and new comprehensions. Together, these constitute Shulman's (1987) Model of Pedagogical Reasoning and Action.

John T. Bruer (1994), in a discussion of Shulman's model of pedagogical content knowledge, indicates that some reform programmes characterize the knowledge base of teaching as consisting of subject-matter knowledge, inter alia. Skilled teaching is dependant upon mastery of the subject-matter; however subject-matter expertise by itself is not sufficient for skilled teaching. Also very critical is the ability to merge smoothly the management of subject-specific ideas and choice of specific teaching methods in dynamic classroom contexts.

Bruer emphasizes the requirement that teachers command their subject matter and pedagogical skills; that they be sensitive to their student audience; and that they be able to integrate these almost at once, to either create a new learning opportunity for students or to remove a learning obstacle.

Since teaching leads to new understanding on the part of both teacher and student, there is little room for teacher ignorance, even in student-centred forms of education where initiative is given to students (Shulman, 1987). Categories of knowledge which underpin the teacher understanding required for student understanding include, as an area of emphasis, pedagogical content knowledge which points to "...distinctive bodies of knowledge for teaching" (Shulman, 1987, p.8). Shulman presents the following definition of pedagogical content knowledge:

> It represents the blending of content and pedagogy into an understanding of how particular topics, problems, or issues are organised, represented, and adapted to the diverse interests and abilities of learners, and presented for instruction. Pedagogical content knowledge is the category most likely to distinguish the understanding of the content specialist from that of the pedagogue. (p.8)

Four major sources for the teaching knowledge base are identified. They are:

1. Scholarship in content disciplines;
2. The materials and settings of the institutionalized educational process (e.g. curricula, textbooks, school organization etc.);
3. Research on schooling and other related phenomena that impact upon teachers' practice; and
4. The wisdom of practice. (Shulman, 1987)

## SCHOLARSHIP IN CONTENT DISCIPLINES

Content knowledge, the first source of the knowledge base, relates to what students should learn in terms of knowledge, understanding, skills and disposition. It rests on the twin pillars of (i) the body of literature and studies in the content areas and (ii) historical and philosophical scholarship on the nature of knowledge in the content areas. The teacher ought also to be familiar with alternative theories of interpretation and criticism in the content areas and their relevance to curricula and teaching issues.

A teacher needs to understand subject matter structures, conceptual organization principles and the principles of inquiry relating to two types of issues in each field of study: the domain's important ideas and skills and how new ideas are added and inadequate ones discarded by the producers of knowledge in the field. The implications of this interpretation of the sources of content knowledge are that teachers must have a depth of understanding of the subjects they teach as well as a breadth of liberal education to enable them to accommodate both old learning and new understanding.

Since the teacher is the primary source of the students' understanding of the subject matter, he or she has a special responsibility in the area of content knowledge. The teacher's manner of communicating understanding to students indicates to them the essential and peripheral elements of a subject. A flexible and multifaceted understanding is required by the teacher in a context of student diversity in order to share alternative perspectives on the same principles or concepts. Since the teacher also, inevitably, transmits to students ideas about the ways in which truth in a field is determined, as well as attitudes and values which inform student understanding, this calls for depth of understanding of subject matter structures, and enthusiasm on the part of the teacher. These aspects of content knowledge are critical in teachers' knowledge base.

## SHULMAN'S (1987) MODEL OF PEDAGOGICAL REASONING AND ACTION

### Comprehension

Shulman (1987) asserts that teaching must be based on understanding. Comprehension, therefore, refers to subject matter structures and ideas within and outside the discipline. Teachers are expected to understand what they teach and even to have several understandings of what they teach. They need to understand the inter-relationship of given ideas within the same subject area and also in other subject areas. They also need to understand the educational goals of the specific area of teaching content knowledge. While the goals of education transcend the understanding of particular texts, the texts are, nonetheless, important to achieving these goals.

## Transformation

The knowledge base of teaching is characterized by the intersection of content and pedagogy. This resides in a teacher's ability to transform content knowledge into powerful pedagogical forms which adapt to students' ability and background variations. Ideas that are understood must be transformed to be taught. In the act of teaching, teachers employ reasoning to communicate subject matter to the learners' minds and motivations.

## Selection

In the selection phase of pedagogical reasoning and action, the teacher moves from representations to instructional forms or methods. An instructional repertoire of approaches or strategies of teaching is assessed. This repertoire can include conventional lectures, cooperative learning, project methods, discovery learning and learning outside the classroom.

## Adaptation and Tailoring to Student Characteristics

Adaptation involves the teacher in fitting material to the students' characteristics. The kinds of questions which are posed in the process of adaptation relate to: (i) relevant aspects of student ability, gender, age, language, culture, motivations, or prior knowledge and skills that are likely to influence how they receive different forms of representation and presentation and (ii) student 'conceptions, misconceptions, expectations, motives, difficulties or strategies' (Shulman, 1987, p.17) that might inform their approach, interpretation, understanding or misunderstanding of the material. Tailoring forms part of the adaptation process. In tailoring, the material is fitted to the specific students in the teachers' class as opposed to students in general. The specific characteristics of the class must be taken into account.

## Instruction

Instruction refers to the variety of teaching acts and entails many critical aspects of pedagogy — management, explanation, discussion, as well as strategies relating to effective direct and heuristic instruction. According to Shulman, there is a strong relationship between comprehension and teaching styles employed. Flexible and interactive teaching techniques are not available to a teacher who does not understand the topic to be taught. Instruction involves teaching acts such as group work presentations, discovery or inquiry instruction, and observable forms of classroom teaching.

## Reflection

Reflection refers to teachers reviewing and critically analyzing their teaching, thus learning from experience. This can be solely on the basis of memory. Teachers review their teaching against what they set out to achieve.

## New Comprehension

Pedagogical Reasoning and Action leads to new comprehension "...both of the purposes and of the subjects to be taught, and also of the students and of the processes of pedagogy themselves" (Shulman, 1987, p.19). Reflection does not lead automatically to new comprehension, however. Rather new comprehension is facilitated by documentation, analysis and discussion.

The processes of Shulman's model are not intended to represent fixed stages, as their sequencing can vary. Indeed, some stages may not even be present at times, or they may be shortened or lengthened.

## THE EMOTIONAL DIMENSION OF PEDAGOGICAL CONTENT KNOWLEDGE

Amidst all the reform work in education and growing literature relating to teachers and students and educational change, there is ignorance or undervaluing of the emotional dimension of teaching (Hargreaves,1998).

The manner in which something is taught affects the feelings and actions of students. This feature of teaching as emotional practice, involving and shaping relationships, requires emotional understanding.

Emotional understanding involves getting into one's own feelings and past emotional experiences in order to relate to those of another. Some of the families of emotions are: anger, sadness, fear, enjoyment, love, surprise, disgust and shame, each having its own family members and particular blends and mutations (Daniel Goleman, 1995).

Inter-subjective emotional understanding occurs when people share similar experiences such as trauma events or personal success (Norman Denzin, 1984). Emotional inter-subjectivity is built through the recurrence of shared feelings and emotions in relationships which have been ongoing. It is also developed through feelings experienced vicariously, by recalling one's own past emotions, and so empathizing with others. It is evident even in the absence of similar experiences or long-term relationships.

Human experience, including learning, is emotional. Education does not take place without the translation of ideas and knowledge into emotion, interest and volition. Learning goes beyond understanding the abstract content of ideas; it also involves self-discovery in relation to new ideas. 'It involves surprise, revelation, delight and sometimes outrage' (Rosiek, 2003, p.399). However, teacher education researchers have given limited consideration to teachers' understanding of student emotion as part of teachers' practical knowledge. Rosiek cites three reasons that render the recognition of teachers' practical knowledge about student emotion desirable: (i) there is empirical evidence that students' emotions influence teachers' decision-making. Teachers respond to students' affective and cognitive response to the subject matter being taught. Quite often teachers must anticipate how specific topics and tasks will impact students' emotional response; (ii) educational scholars from a broad range of disciplines have declared that emotions feature prominently in the learning process; (iii) there is a moral necessity to promote responsiveness to students' emotional experience of learning and particularly so in respect of students who are on the cultural fringes of school culture, or who are very unsuccessful or disadvantaged in any other way. It is necessary to document and analyse teachers' understanding of students' emotional response to curriculum content (Rosiek, 2003). This will supplement research focused primarily on the cognitive dimensions of teachers' practical knowledge.

There are other arguments in support of emotional understanding in education. These concern teachers relating to students and empathizing with their life circumstances; being perceptive of their emotional engagement with subject matter and understanding the classroom's social dynamics, that is, whether the classroom's social climate was facilitating or inhibiting learning (Mc Caughtry, 2004).

A shortcoming of pedagogical content knowledge theory and research has been its tendency 'to eliminate teacher knowledge of student emotion from analyses of how teachers think students learn' (Rosiek, 2003, p.33). This perspective is also shared by Mc Caughtry (2004). Indeed, teacher knowledge of student emotion is seen to be integral to understanding student learning. Teacher interpretation of and response to student emotion are key aspects of their pedagogical content knowledge. Understanding students' emotions may be as pivotal to effective decision making about content, curriculum and pedagogy as the understanding teachers have of students' prior knowledge, motor skill development or knowledge and skill acquisition patterns (Mc Caughtry, 2004).

The findings of a collaborative research process on pedagogical content knowledge, over a ten-year period and involving both intern teachers and more experienced teachers, focused on the ways scaffolding for student learning is provided by teachers (Rosiek, 2003). Scaffolding is described as an output of Vygotsky's (1997) social psychology which refers to the ways in which teachers assist students to cognitively frame their learning experience. Within this research process, scaffolding with the aim of influencing students' emotional responses to an idea, or emotional scaffolding, generated considerable interest and discussions. Documenting and analyzing the practice of emotional scaffolding brings an emotional dimension to the understanding of pedagogical content knowledge (Rosiek, 2003). A prominent part of teachers' efforts to 'transform' subject matter is their attention to student emotion (Shulman, 1987). In order to do this, teachers use their understanding of students' cultures, backgrounds and attitudes to schooling. The emotional dimension of pedagogical content knowledge is, therefore, shaped by culture and local context (Rosiek, 2003).

## An Emotional Scaffolding Typology

Distinctive approaches to emotional scaffolding suggest implications for ongoing debates concerning the extent to which the practical knowledge of teachers can be generalized or is dependent upon context (Rosiek, 2003). Two principal patterns of emotional scaffolding, as reported by Rosiek, are discussed below. These relate to the kind of emotion and teachers' choices for addressing students' emotional response to subject matter.

### The kind of emotion

According to findings of the research process reported by Rosiek, teachers, in some cases, tried to lower the intensity of unconstructive emotions about a topic or concept. In other cases, they tried to increase constructive emotions about an idea or subject. All uncomfortable emotions were not deemed *unconstructive* emotions.

Discomforting emotions such as anger or sadness can often serve to draw students more into the subject matter being taught. Unconstructive emotions are those which distract students from the subject matter content or otherwise inhibit their learning. *Constructive emotion*, on the other hand, refers not to just any positive emotion, but rather to emotions which pull students more closely into the important aspects of the subject matter being taught.

### Teacher's treatment of students' emotional response to the subject matter

Teachers offered emotional scaffolding either explicitly, addressing students' emotions directly, or implicitly, that is, by avoiding discussion of student emotions but nonetheless planning for them in a lesson.

Since human emotions are complicated, these distinctions between types of emotional scaffolding are considered to be rudimentary, and would need to be refined by further research. Avoiding oversimplification of the emotional dimension of teaching requires critical attention to the role of context in influencing emotion in the classroom and the ability of teachers to interpret that emotion. Emotional scaffolding was made possible by teachers having context-specific knowledge. Scholarly attention to assisting students in building emotional as well as cognitive relations to what they are learning is needed (Rosiek, 2003). Future research in this area potentially holds significant implications for teacher education curricula. It is possible that there exists a noteworthy overlap of the ways in which teachers think about student emotion, subject matter specifics and teaching's social and cultural context. This warrants attention to integrating these three areas in teacher education curricula (Rosiek, 2003).

Another study reports one teacher's emotional understanding and the ways in which such understanding merged with her knowledge of content, curriculum and pedagogy (Mc Caughtry, 2004). These included the teacher listening to her students' feelings about their learning, which helped her to assess how they were advancing through the content; knowing how students were affiliating emotionally with content, other students and teachers in the process of learning; and understanding the unique perspectives of students of different ethnic groups, different skill abilities and different temperaments.

## THE REFORMED VISION OF THE CURRICULUM

Lorrie Shepard (2000), American educator and educational administrator, makes observations about the cognitive revolution that are relevant to the discussion of the pedagogy of the TTEA. These observations include the following:

1. The cognitive revolution reintroduced the concept of mind.
2. The cognitive revolution interprets learning as involving active mental construction and sense making, which contrasts with mechanistic theories of knowledge acquisition of the past.
3. Learning is either enabled or impacted by existing knowledge structures and beliefs. This underscores the importance of content knowledge and mastery of that knowledge by teachers. However, the cognitive alone does not produce learning as beliefs can serve as emotional filters to either enable or impede learning.

4. Self-monitoring and awareness about when and how to use skills contribute to intelligent thought.
5. A principled and coherent way of thinking and representing problems as opposed to accumulation of information constitutes 'expertise' in a field of study.

These elements of the reformed vision of the curriculum can assist educators in the formulation of an educational strategy for teaching the TTEA.

## HUMAN DEVELOPMENT, HISTORY TEACHING AND CITIZENSHIP

### Human Development

*Learning: The Treasure Within, the Report to UNESCO of the International Commission on Education for the Twenty-first Century* acknowledges that every part of education contributes to human development and that development should ensure "... the full flowering of the human being and not as a means of production" (p.79). The Report states further that people's understanding of themselves and others must form part of responsible development, so that they are able to participate in collective societal undertakings. It cites some of the key dimensions of the state of human development as presented in the *UNDP Human Development Report* (1995):

(i) The process of human development enlarges people's choices and among the essential choices are the acquisition of knowledge and access to resources necessary for a decent standard of living;
(ii) Additional choices that are generally highly valued are in the domain of enhancing the quality of human lives. They encompass political, economic and social freedom; opportunities for being creative and productive and the enjoyment of personal self-respect and guaranteed human rights;
(iii) Human development addresses all societal issues (economic growth, trade, employment, political freedom or cultural

values) from the perspective of people. This implies that education must go beyond narrow utilitarian purposes and 'should serve to make human beings not the means but the justification of development.' (Learning: The Treasure Within, p.80)

## The four pillars of education

*Learning: The Treasure Within* also elaborates upon four pillars considered to be the foundation of all education. These pillars are: (i) learning to know; (ii) learning to do; (iii) learning to live together; and (iv) learning to be. These four pillars must also be seen as contributing to human development. In particular, learning to live together and learning to be can be greatly facilitated by teaching the TTEA. Learning to live together is achieved through an understanding of others; appreciating interdependence and learning to manage conflicts with due regard for 'the values of pluralism, mutual understanding and peace' (p.97). Learning to be is supportive of the concept of education as 'an inner journey facilitating the continuing maturing of the personality'.

## History teaching and citizenship

René Rémond (1998), French political scientist, expresses the view that respecting historical truth and the rules of historical method can ensure that the propagation of history and of research findings can contribute to greater social cohesion which should be among the ultimate aims of any education system. Rémond identifies benefits history can offer and reasons for history having an important role to play in the education of citizens for the twenty-first century. He states that history can make possible a clearer understanding of the place of the individual in society. The significance of the collective experience of humankind should be clearly exposed for the benefit of the young. The transition of societies from violence to the rule of law is an outcome of history that remains insecure and the preservation of such outcomes requires the full support and active participation of all members of society.

Rémond advocates that historians make value judgements in the teaching of history and describe actions for what they are, pointing the finger of blame. He expresses the view that 'some actions merit condemnation, some practices are reprehensible and history cannot remain absolutely neutral' (p.347). History, therefore, has a very important contribution to make to society. However, he argues that teachers have not been prepared to make such judgements and, further, may not feel themselves entitled to do so as their own judgement may not be either sound or firm enough. He thus argues for preparing teachers to fulfil this role of history:

> Hence the basic problem is to train teachers in such a way that they will be able to draw out from history the lessons it furnishes. An education system that fails to provide teachers with such training is clearly failing in its duty by neglecting not only to give instruction in citizenship but also to develop abilities and aptitudes in individuals that are part and parcel of their personalities (p.348).

Rémond offers guiding principles for teaching history and influencing citizenship that also appear to be compatible with the concept of human development. He stipulates that:

(i) history should not become a means of indoctrination or conditioning;
(ii) teachers must be allowed time to think and must acquire a deeper appreciation of their potentially vital contribution to a more profound reflection upon social or political philosophy;
(iii) history teaches respect for complexity and the discovery of complexity is an essential aspect of training in citizenship;
(iv) knowledge of history is useful to people engaged in action. It enables differentiation between what has been inherited from the past, and what can and cannot be changed. Memory assists people in determining where they fit in;
(v) history facilitates a pluralist outlook as one is led to go outside of one's tradition to discover others that deserve consideration;

## SIGNIFICANCE OF AND LIMITATIONS OF THIS STUDY

The significance of this book resides in the contribution it represents towards a better understanding of what is involved in teaching about a historical phenomenon which had a major impact on the making of the New World and on the underdevelopment of another space – the continent of Africa. It is hoped that the book will facilitate an appreciation of issues and challenges relating to the pedagogy of the TTEA as understood through the teaching practice of particular teachers and educators from the three geographic regions of the world which were the major players in the TTEA: Africa, the Americas/Caribbean and Europe. It can also inform the development of teacher education curricula that can, more effectively, prepare teachers to teach this subject to establish for young people its relevance to their lives. Teaching the TTEA in a manner that is empowering, notwithstanding the human tragedy that this history represents, can serve to promote human development, thus representing a form of reparation for past wrongs.

## SUMMARY

Chapter 2 has presented the background and conceptual framework which allow for a fuller understanding of the context within which the contents of this book are located. It is a context in which UNESCO's response to breaking the silence surrounding the historical phenomenon of the TTEA serves as a major initiative in modernity. The chapter has also discussed the guiding elements, and the conceptual framework informing the discussion of the pedagogy of the TTEA.

CHAPTER 3

# ISSUES AND CHALLENGES

## INTRODUCTION

An African proverb teaches us that until lions have their own historians, tales of the hunt will always glorify the hunter. This proverb, in its subtlety, signals the importance of those who have been victimized or oppressed developing the skills to present their own stories, their own histories, not so they will glorify themselves but to ensure the truth is told or at least that the story of those who have been wronged will be respected, preserved and the lessons learned passed on. Teaching the TTEA is a present-day exercise ensuring the history of the forced migration of millions of Africans over hundreds of years, their enslavement and that of their offspring, and the legacies of this is passed on. It is on teachers, in both formal and non-formal education systems, that the responsibility falls to tell the story. To do so effectively teachers need the guidance of historians who research and write the history which they in turn must interpret in the classroom. It is also to teachers that we must turn in order to understand the issues and challenges of the pedagogy of the TTEA in today's world.

## EDUCATIONAL CONTEXTS RELATING TO THE PEDAGOGY OF THE TRANSATLANTIC TRADE IN ENSLAVED AFRICANS

The author's understanding of the issues and challenges of the pedagogy of the TTEA is based on the findings of qualitative research, conducted over the period February, 2001 to October, 2002 in the following geographic regions and countries:

1. **Americas/Caribbean:** Barbados, Brazil, Dominican Republic, Jamaica, Trinidad and Tobago, USA
2. **Africa:** Benin, Senegal, the Gambia
3. **Europe:** England, Denmark

## Case Study Approach, Sampling and Sources of Data Collection

Interviewees in the study on which this work is based met the criterion of teaching the historiography of the TTEA in the context of the UNESCO 'Transatlantic Slave Trade Education Project', or being directly involved in the coordination or administration of the Project at school level or at the national level or were involved in the Project as students. Using a multi-site case study approach 39 persons were interviewed including 33 teachers, two administrators and four secondary school students, two in Denmark and two in Jamaica. Of the teachers interviewed, two of them taught the TTEA at secondary level, but were not involved in the UNESCO Project, one in New Orleans, USA and one in Trinidad and Tobago.

The purpose of the interpretation of a case study is to facilitate understanding of an issue, either as a result of what one can learn from the case or through its application to other cases.

The research tradition of phenomenology, and in particular the psychological approach as described by John Creswell (1998), infused this inquiry. The concern was with the meaning and description of the lived experience of a phenomenon for several individuals. General meanings are derived from individual descriptions. Phenomenology represents a search for wisdom.

The phenomenological report enables the reader to better understand the essence of the experience. While Creswell discusses the 'essence' of the experience in the sense of all experiences being underpinned by a single unifying meaning, the author's search for essence focused on the dominant ways in which participants in the study experienced teaching the TTEA as a lived experience.

Various sources of information were drawn upon in the conduct of the inquiry and in the synthesis of findings: texts and other writings on the TTEA, including articles in the press, data obtained from interviewees (teachers, administrators, students) and a small sample of students' written assignments. Findings were considered using the lens of different theories from the literature discussed in Chapter 2.

Most of the interviews were conducted, audio-taped and transcribed in English. In a few cases, interviews were conducted by the author in French (Benin, Senegal) and Spanish (in Brazil the teachers interviewed understood Spanish) and then translated into English. In the case of Brazil, the author was assisted by a teacher who spoke Portuguese, Spanish and English and who facilitated communication with interviewees. The author employed foreign language graduates of The University of the West Indies who are practising foreign language teachers at secondary school and university levels to translate and transcribe interviews from French, Spanish and Portuguese into English.

In keeping with the traditions of case studies and phenomenological research, in-depth, semi-structured interviews were conducted both with individual teachers and with teachers in focus groups. All were face-to-face interviews with one exception where the interview was conducted via email. The use of focus groups allowed access to the perspectives of a larger group when there were time constraints. Focus groups seemed to bring a greater level of energy and sharing to the discussions.

Teachers interviewed taught history, social studies, African studies, sociology, special education and library studies and had between five and 30 years teaching experience. Several had received higher education training, in some cases up to the level of the master's degree. One university lecturer was at the time completing his Doctor of Philosophy degree in education and one administrator held a Doctor of Philosophy degree in African studies.

## Issues Relating to General Educational Contexts

### The United Kingdom

The administrator interviewed in the UK explained that teaching the TTEA was not seen as an area of great importance in the UK and that this was reflected in the national curriculum for history where it was incorporated under the Industrial Revolution component. The subject was not compulsory content. Teachers did not have to teach the slave trade in history or in any other subject. It was presented as an example in one or two of the units in the history curriculum for 11 to 14 year olds. Teachers were described as being under pressure to fulfil government requirements. As in the Caribbean, students in the UK could drop history at age 14, just before they went into their fourth year of secondary level education. If they continued with history between 14 and 16 years of age, they would be exposed to the TTEA to some degree. The subject was an area that could be easily overlooked, given the structure of the curriculum, unless there were dedicated teachers who, in turn, were supported by their schools. A new national curriculum was described as seeking to incorporate national perspectives more than the old curriculum and to present a wider picture, presenting the realities behind a field of study such as history and framed in an international context.

While there is a wealth of information about the TTEA in the UK, there was a perception of a collective amnesia about the slave trade in that country and knowledge of it was considered to be just for the academic world. It is not accessible to students, and teachers, as a result, felt alienated from it.

Though at the level of the national curriculum serious constraints existed for teaching the history of the TTEA, non-governmental agencies such as Antislavery International produce materials on past and present forms of slavery and make them available to teachers.

In one teacher education programme in the UK (at which two teacher educators were interviewed), seven hours were spent on the TTEA out of a forty-hour scheme of work in history for a term. Essentially, therefore, one day was spent on the TTEA for the duration of the Post-Graduate Certificate of Education (PGCE) course in history. Teachers were expected to go into the school system on the basis of this one-day training experience. While this is certainly better than no training at all, it is certainly inadequate given the scope and the challenging nature of the subject matter.

## Denmark

At the time that the study was undertaken, teachers in Denmark had considerable freedom in selecting what they teach. Teachers had no obligation to teach the TTEA but could choose to do so if they considered it to be relevant. They enjoyed a great deal of freedom in determining what was relevant to their students while working within certain guidelines. From the perspective of the Danish teachers involved in the UNESCO Associated Schools 'Transatlantic Slave Trade Education Project' the subject of the TTEA was hardly known in Denmark. Nothing was taught systematically and no primary sources were used at all. Slavery was dealt with only in connection with the cotton growing of the American South and the conflict with the industrialized North. Failure to teach the TTEA was explained by a seeming lack of relevance to Danish identity and the fact of the topic not being a specific requirement of the curriculum.

Accessing primary sources to pursue the subject was described as being difficult. Some of the available printed materials on the subject were considered to be exclusively scientific works intended for an academic audience and, therefore, would not be suitable for the purpose of teaching. Primary material was viewed as being difficult to consult because of the need to decipher old documents and to make the old Danish language accessible. The teachers were of the view that the subject was difficult to approach. A great deal of visual material was thought to exist but there was the question of collecting it and organizing it into themes. This was seen as requiring time and money and as not possible for a single teacher to do. What was believed to be more realistic was the collection of such visual material from all over the world for exchange among teachers.

The teachers were of the view that an effectively run network of UNESCO Associated Schools could help to alleviate the difficulty of producing and making accessible relevant and pedagogically edited teaching material for different age groups. The meaningful use of the technical possibilities of the Internet was also considered a possible solution to the sourcing of materials, as was the production of CDs. These teachers proposed the compilation of CDs with suggestions for a single lesson, a whole day, a fortnight or a year-theme for different age groups. Teachers could either use the CDs as produced or adapt the material to their own teaching plan. They considered CDs very cheap, easy to distribute and very flexible to use.

Within the context of the UNESCO Project in Denmark, while written material provided the foundation for a great deal of the work, students and teachers had been approaching the subject of the TTEA from different angles. Art, literature, poetry, music and theatre had been used to place slavery and slave trading into new perspectives. A great deal of use was made of guest teachers, artists and musicians. However, it was recognized that it was the use of information technology which facilitated the goal of working on the subject from a global perspective. Some schools have started teaching it within the context of the UNESCO Project.

The need was identified for the production of materials illustrating ways in which individuals can take a stand on slave trading and slavery in other places in the world. The view was expressed that such materials should include descriptions by 'victims' about what happened and what effect such incidents had on their present day societies.

## *Africa: Benin*

In Benin several non-governmental organizations such as Amnesty International and human rights bodies invested in the education system. The education system of itself had become more open to programmes such as the UNESCO Associated Schools 'Transatlantic Slave Trade Education Project'. Within the wider society there was also much discussion about a resurgence of slavery, though, it was explained, this was not the case in respect of the trade. According to the Beninese teacher the resurgence of slavery manifested itself with respect to children — poverty-stricken children sold into slavery, child exploitation, paedophilia and sex slavery.

Under the umbrella of the UNESCO Project the following activities were undertaken:

- Periodic outings were organized to Ouidah, Allada and Abomey, three big focal cities in the history of the TTEA.
- Conferences and symposia were organized in the high schools and secondary schools involved, especially on the cultural days.

- Cultural activities were organized and included poetry writing, workshops on plastic arts, dance, short ballets and drawing competitions on the TTEA, thus enabling students to demonstrate their creativity.
- A simplified form of the UNESCO questionnaire to assess students' knowledge and attitudes relating to the TTEA was developed and every year students were given a pre and post test, using this questionnaire.
- The second Sunday of every month was observed as Repentance Day for youths and civil society.
- The subject of the TTEA had been integrated into the new syllabuses that were being reviewed and trial tested in Benin.

In the implementation of these activities there was close collaboration with the following:

- Civil society organizations fighting against slavery and human rights groups such as Amnesty International.
- The Ouidah Museum and Management Committee of Historic Sites in Ouidah.
- The Ouidah Secondary Schools and the Frčres Bouvier Institutions in Haiti that had developed an inter-cultural twinning programme.

In spite of the keen interest manifested at the Benin National Workshop for the Project, the Ministry of Education and Scientific Research in that country had not given it any concrete support. There was no formal and concerted action at the school level for the implementation of the Project and the implementation of the National Action Plan for the Project was hindered by inertia on the part of political and administrative authorities. Further, the austere schools budgets could not facilitate Project implementation at the school level.

## *Africa:* **Senegal**

According to the Senegalese teacher interviewed, slavery was taught at all levels of the Senegalese education system: primary, secondary and higher education. Teaching focused on causes and mechanisms of the trade and the consequences in Africa, the Americas and in Europe. Students did not have manuals and resource materials were described as rare. Materials provided by UNESCO were considered to be very useful. Some of the sections of the main texts were extracted and given to teachers for easier access by learners.

Educational approaches employed in Senegal included project work on the TTEA; presentations by resource persons, drama, poetry, film shows and visits to historic sites, such as Gorée Island; viewing of the film *Roots* and extracts of a television programme on the 'Memory Ring' in all the schools involved in the Project; exchange activities among the schools involved in inter-school meetings; symposia; quiz competitions; poetry recitals; drama; Internet surfing and research using the national archives and the Senegalese Association of History and Geography Teachers.

Teachers lost much time preparing lessons. Visits to sites required means that were not available. Insufficient means proved a major obstacle to all teacher initiatives to produce education research material.

The UNESCO project was described as being important in Senegal to enable:

- An active pedagogy
- A personal commitment of students
- The provision of various and useful documentation
- An indispensable support for a meaningful education
- The development of interdisciplinarity

## Africa: *The Gambia*

The national coordinator for the UNESCO Associated Schools 'Transatlantic Slave Trade Education Project' in the Gambia, in her report to the April, 2001 sub-regional meeting, gave an overview of the Project implementation in the Gambia.

There were field trips to James Island, Albreda, Fort Bullen and the Slave Museum. A history lecture on the TTEA and the Gambia's involvement in the trade was given. A cleaning up exercise was held in Albreda. Not only did this experience provide an opportunity for social interaction among the youth from different participating schools and regions, it also created awareness of the actual geographic route of the TTEA within the Gambia.

At the school level, classroom lectures, concerts, fashion shows, debates, symposia, school assemblies, video shows and talks had been used as media not only for teaching and learning about the TTEA but also as sensitization activities for the wider public. Visits to the national museum were also organized. Students were given research assignments at documentation centres and libraries. Fund raising activities were held and the proceeds from one of these activities were used to facilitate the participation of the Gambia in the Project's youth forum, held in Badagry, Nigeria.

Financial resources were limited. The Primary and Higher Teachers' Certificate Course Content did not have much material on the TTEA, thus student teachers' knowledge at the first level of training was inadequate. Teacher training activities were described as being short term and ad hoc but a series of activities had been planned.

## *The Americas/Caribbean:* **New Orleans, the United States of America**

Three teachers in New Orleans were interviewed. Two of them taught at a public secondary school located in Central City, New Orleans with the students coming from two major housing developments in the area. The other taught at an elite, 'mainly white' high school for girls described as a technology school. The public secondary school was described as being in crisis because of students' low score performance. The UNESCO Associated Schools 'Transatlantic Slave Trade Education Project' was integrated into the social studies curriculum and was considered an alternative way to help students perform better. The curriculum used for the school's participation in the Project was written by a senior education administrator in the New Orleans public schools system who also served as the New Orleans coordinator for the Project.

The library of this school included an African Studies Report Centre. Resources to support the Project were, therefore, housed in the school library. There were computers in the classrooms with access to the Internet. Students were described as having 'tough' lives, given the poverty in which many of them lived. As a result of this, according to the teachers interviewed, it was not easy for them to feel compassion for others.

Particular features of the school's student population were that 180 out of 400 students were described as special needs 'crack children', that is, their parents were drug addicts so that many of them had to fend for themselves. Children with special needs were unable to follow the regular programme for the entire school day and needed remediation. In some cases students were not sure whether they would see their mother when they got home as she might be engaged in prostitution to get money to buy drugs. They were not sure of getting food as a strange person might be in the house eating their food. Children were unattended by their parents and teachers had to do some very basic things for them.

The curriculum used to teach the TTEA in the New Orleans public school included thematic areas which did not form part of the UNESCO Project, for example: 'The Making of the Diaspora', 'African Louisiana History' and 'Sugarcane Culture'. Curricula, produced by the New Orleans Department of Public Education, were adapted for use in the context of the UNESCO Project. Part of this curriculum dealt with transatlantic enslavement. It included mathematical equations dealing with how many Africans were on the ships, averaging how many Africans were lost during the voyage and how many Africans arrived. Such information was seen to have an impact on students. The Middle Passage was presented as the middle component of the Triangular Trade. The curriculum also addressed the establishment of the diaspora and African America, particularly African Louisiana.

It was quite clear that teaching African history and the TTEA was supported by the Department of New Orleans Public Schools with the senior administrator himself playing a key and active role. In the New Orleans public school involved in the Project, one would, therefore, expect fewer constraints for teaching this subject arising from the boundaries set by the official curriculum.

## The Americas/Caribbean: Brazil

As in the case of the other countries, Brazil adopted an interdisciplinary approach to teaching the TTEA within the framework of the UNESCO Project. The Project was viewed as an opportunity to re-establish the study of one of the most important chapters in world history, the consequences of which were considered to be still present in Brazil. Subject areas identified for teaching the TTEA were mathematics and geometry, religious education (the influence of African culture on religion and customs in Brazilian society), science, chemistry, biology, geography, Portuguese, history and foreign languages.

At a national meeting of the Project in Maranaho in northeast Brazil, participating schools put on impressive displays on the TTEA in Brazil, including a very sensitive theatrical presentation by one of the schools.

## The Americas/Caribbean: The English-speaking Caribbean — Barbados, Jamaica, Trinidad and Tobago

The case of the English-speaking Caribbean appeared to be unique because of the provisions of the Caribbean Examinations Council (CXC) for the development of regional curricula and examinations, often with extensive input from academics from the University of the West Indies (UWI). Barbados, Jamaica, and Trinidad and Tobago, therefore, had within their school curricula, at the national level, a common framework for the study of Caribbean history and the TTEA. In this case, however, the limitations which existed for teaching the subject were particularly at the lower level of the secondary school system. In many secondary schools, social studies had replaced history and where history was taught it was not certain that students would be exposed to the TTEA. However, students who pursued history as a discipline at the upper secondary school level were exposed to the TTEA topic and to African history.

According to CXC, the objectives of its history syllabus are informed by the nature of history and students' perceived needs and interests. The core syllabus was designed to provide students with an overview of major areas and trends in Caribbean history with which it was believed every student of Caribbean history should be familiar. In both the core and thematic areas of the syllabus slavery occupied a prominent place. The core syllabus provided for students acquiring knowledge and understanding of the following, inter alia:

1. The causes and consequences of interaction within and among the major groups in the region, namely: indigenous peoples, Africans, Asians and Europeans.
2. Slavery and emancipation in the Caribbean.

Topics which constituted the core aspects of the CXC history syllabus which addressed the subject of the TTEA were:

- The economic revolution and the coming of enslaved Africans
- Slave resistance
- Emancipation and apprenticeship
- Coming of the Chinese, Europeans, Indians and enslaved Africans
- The existence of the peasantry up to the end of the nineteenth century

The ten thematic areas of the CXC history syllabus were all linked to the subject of slavery and its impact in the Caribbean; however, four of these themes addressed the subject of slavery directly. They were:

- Caribbean Economy and Slavery
- Resistance and Revolt
- Movements Toward Emancipation
- Adjustments to Emancipation, 1838-1876

The Caribbean Advanced Proficiency Examination (CAPE) history syllabus was geared toward the preparation of students for advanced tertiary education in the study of history and other disciplines. The syllabus presented the Caribbean and the Atlantic region as a theatre for the creation of some foundations of the modern world. As is to be expected at this level, there was a more in-depth treatment of slavery and the African contribution to the New World. The CXC CAPE syllabus has been critiqued by some UWI academics in Trinidad and Tobago, a multicultural society, as being too Afrocentric.

## *The Americas/Caribbean: The Dominican Republic*

The TTEA was not taught as part of the school curriculum in the Dominican Republic. Slavery was mentioned only in very short paragraphs in school texts. The interviewee from this country, a tertiary education lecturer in history, cultural activist and poet expressed the view that there was a great deal of work to be done on school texts and in the school curriculum.

### TEXTBOOKS

School textbooks should convey historical reality as presented by recent academic writers considered to be the best in their field. Judgement of a work of history should be informed by what it is setting out to do and by the level on which it is aiming to operate (Marwick, 1989). The following four criteria are proposed for assessing a history textbook:

1. A textbook should convey an understanding of the pronouncements of the major authorities and should reflect any unresolved controversy.
2. A textbook should be informed by the most recent significant discoveries of contemporary researchers. Marwick (1989) also promotes the viewpoint that 'no textbook should present interpretations which run contrary to the considered opinions of the recognised experts' (p.266). This is likely to be contentious in view of omissions and marginalizations by recognized experts.
3. Matters which are scholarly, either too technical or too detailed, ought not to command space in a textbook.
4. A textbook should communicate some of the excitement of history.

Five different categories of history textbooks are identified and these are:

(i) The *outline* type which summarizes more comprehensive histories.
(ii) The *condensed* text which is an abridged, more digestible form of the outline type.
(iii) The *pupil-oriented* type which is more demanding of the student than of the teacher with more illustrations and questions to guide study.
(iv) The *era* approach type presenting limited periods of time in greater detail.
(v) The *supplementary readers* emphasizing the story element in history and which includes some primary source materials (Marsden, 2001).

External examination syllabuses exercise an increasingly important influence on textbook content in the USA and Britain (Marsden, 2001).

Marsden uses various lenses to assess textbooks. For the purposes of this discussion, emphasis will be placed on language, bias and stereotyping in textbooks.

## The Language and Degrees of Bias and Stereotyping in Textbooks

In terms of language, factors to be considered in assessing history textbooks include accessibility to students of the age group targeted; vocabulary level; conceptual difficulty; and organization which deals with, for example, manipulating structures such as summarizing key concepts in advance and judicious use of subheadings. The use of technical prose in textbooks is another area of concern as complex information which is new to the reader and densely packed inhibits meaningful learning and lowers motivation (Marsden, 2001).

Writers are seen to be a source of bias in textbooks through their choice of sources and the transmission of their own values. Over-reliance on certain explanatory paradigms within the discipline of history is seen as a source of bias. Age, gender, national or regional location and ethnic or social class affiliation are other factors seen to contribute to authors' bias and prejudice.

A result of the increased awareness of and complaints about

stereotyping is the avoidance, on the part of publishers, of controversial topics. Critical of the tendency in many modern textbooks to seek to be neutral, Marsden (2001) seems to favour the approach of the nineteenth century authors to make valuable judgements rather than sit on the fence. In support of this position, he quotes Rémond (1998, p.347) who advocated that historians:

> ...must describe actions for what they are and, if necessary, point the finger or blame, thus distancing themselves both from a certain positivist tradition which denied itself the right to judge and from a certain contemporary attitude to cultural identities which verges on relativism (p.132).

Types of bias and prejudice are (i) religious bias and prejudice (ii) national and racial stereotyping (iii) gender bias and prejudice and (iv) social class and age (Marsden, 2001). Bias in history teaching is considered to be most clearly visible in matters of religion, as in an inadequate treatment of non-Christian religions, for example, Islam.

While there has been an increased representation of women in history books and an avoidance of extreme sexist language, texts continue to reveal a gender imbalance due, in part, to the predominance of male authors. In the USA it was found that there was a marginalization of the historical contribution of women; that there was an even more peripheral treatment of coloured women; but that there was relatively little overt sexist language, though still a need for continuing scrutiny in this regard (Marsden, 2001).

Concern has also been raised about the dissemination of middle-class lifestyles and values as the norm as well as about the small proportion of elderly people depicted in textbooks.

## SUMMARY

The experience of focus group interviews in Barbados, Brazil, Jamaica,1 and Trinidad and Tobago illustrated the way in which teachers meeting in groups to discuss and share experiences could, in itself, provide valuable learning opportunities especially for less experienced teachers. The interviews and ensuing discussions were animated and seemed to generate enthusiasm.

The importance of teachers' interest and enthusiasm for particular subjects was especially evident in the case of Europe and the USA where dedicated teachers — seemingly sensitive to issues of social justice, equality and the empowerment of their students and all aspects of human development — made a focused effort to integrate black history and the TTEA into their classroom teaching.

Teachers' interests proved to be significant in terms of influencing what was taught, outside of what would normally be expected within the curriculum, based on the concept of the relevance of content knowledge to students' perceived needs and interests. Not required to teach black history or the TTEA, they did so essentially because of their personal values and concern to fill the gaps in the offerings of the official curriculum where the trade, its causes, consequences and legacies were concerned, so as to ensure their students' appreciation of the significance of this phenomenon in world history. Teachers' personal experiences also appeared to be important in their approach to teaching the TTEA topic.

Even in the context of Denmark and what appeared to be a flexible system of education, there remained some basic boundaries within which teachers had to function if they were to be accountable to the relevant educational authorities. The educational context of the UK highlighted the issue of teachers' lack of preparation to teach the subject, and the strategies which conscious teacher educators were obliged to use to provide trainee teachers with a minimum amount of pedagogical content knowledge. The two teacher educators interviewed expressed great concern that teachers be equipped with the necessary knowledge and skills to teach black history.

In the Caribbean, students of history spent considerably more time TTEA on the subject of enslavement which was examined, and in the New Orleans public secondary school, a specific block of time was dedicated to the subject in the second, third and fourth quarters of the academic year, in the context of the Project.

While the great benefits of information technology resources were particularly evident in the USA, sensitive and knowledgeable teachers also emerged as being among the most valuable resources of these schools. This was particularly evident in the case of schools where the students involved in the Project, in general, come from socio-economically disadvantaged areas, a reality about which their teachers seemed very aware and concerned. However, socio-economic difficulties were not exclusive to schools with minority groups or significant black populations as teachers in the UK also spoke of white students living in poverty.

CHAPTER 4

# TEACHERS' PRESENTATION OF CONTENT KNOWLEDGE

What is the content knowledge of the major thematic areas of the history of the transatlantic trade in enslaved Africans (TTEA) taught by the teachers interviewed? The thematic areas examined in this study were:

1. Supply of enslaved Africans to the New World
2. How enslaved Africans were used
3. Slavery in Brazil
4. Africans in Western Europe in the eighteenth century
5. The Triangular Trade
6. The role of European countries in the TTEA
7. Major slave trading ports
8. The duration of the slave trade
9. How enslaved Africans were shipped
10. The Middle Passage
11. The number of enslaved Africans a typical slave ship crossing the Atlantic carried
12. Maroons
13. Toussaint L'Ouverture
14. Why the slave trade to the Caribbean was stopped
15. The human tragedy of the TTEA

This chapter provides the responses by the interviewees on each thematic area. The intention is to show the range of responses as they reflect areas of focus, limitations and approaches.

## The Americas and the Caribbean

The interviewees in this region comprise educators from Barbados, Jamaica, Trinidad and Tobago, Brazil, the USA and the Dominican Republic.

### Supply of Enslaved Africans to the New World

In Barbados, teachers tried to show the existence of slavery in both Africa and Europe. Teacher I (ii) treated with the people who were involved in the supply of enslaved Africans: the Europeans and the Africans. She explained that this question of the supply of enslaved Africans as chattel – robbing them of their dignity as human beings – and the involvement of Africans in the trade, could be very upsetting for students. In order to deal with this idea the teacher explained that the trade must be viewed 'as part of a war'. She felt this theme required considerable attention to deal with the tendency in the literature to lead learners to 'see it as their forefathers sold them into slavery...' This encourages self-blame and, consequently, she works hard at dealing with the affective dimension of learners' classroom experience relating to this subject.

In Jamaica, Teacher J (i) indicated that enslaved Africans first came with the Spaniards in the capacity of soldiers. In her research, she found that the Spaniards brought the first set of enslaved Africans 'to help them conquer the islands and then as the slave trade developed they came directly by the Middle Passage.' She taught her students that most enslaved Africans were taken from West Africa, noting that some areas participated in the trade more than others.

Teacher T (i) in Trinidad and Tobago, explored this theme in the context of market networks within Africa and the impact of the trade in re-orienting the African economic system to service the Atlantic economic system.

The educator from the Dominican Republic also approached teaching the supply of enslaved Africans by tracing the slavery system as it was known in ancient history. He began with the slavery system before 1492, with the economic system and the existence of slavery all over the world.

## How Enslaved Africans were Used

Teachers in Barbados and Jamaica examined the roles of enslaved Africans on the plantation and their categorization as domestic slaves and field slaves. Students in Barbados, thinking of themselves in that situation, said they would have preferred to be domestic slaves since they got 'more perks than the field slaves.'

Teacher I (ii) in Barbados also concentrated on slave owners keeping the enslaved Africans divided, and on exploitation, including the sexual exploitation of children and women (including wives) and the disruption this caused in the family life of enslaved peoples.

One teacher in Jamaica taught the pyramid for the classification of the enslaved Africans and the social hierarchy this created. Enslaved Africans, she explained, were divided into domestic slaves, field slaves and artisans, the latter considered the most important because of the type of work they did.

Teacher S in the USA used a visit to the Laura Plantation on the outskirts of New Orleans to effectively illustrate the work of the little children in the system. She taught that some had to get up early in the morning and ring the bells, that some worked in the fields, and some in houses.

The Brazilian teachers first worked on slavery in general then looked at the specific case of slavery in the Americas. A focus was placed on the diverse uses of slave labour — that the black person in Brazil appeared to be a social agent and a 'history constructor as well'. As one teacher put it, 'they brought something from their culture and used it to build something here'. These teachers dealt with the social diversity of the enslaved Africans and examined the African contribution to the entire Brazilian economy. In Brazil, the main sectors which made use of slave labour were the sugar, mining and coffee industries. They explained that recent studies have shown that in the mining sector there were three categories of slave labour: those who did the heavy work, the domestics and those who did the selling, including prostitution. Male slaves were used for breeding, as with domesticated animals, to produce stronger slaves. The statement was made that 'the Brazilian economy was built on the shoulders of the slave, they were involved in all sectors.'

## Slavery in Brazil

Teacher N in the USA dealt with slavery in Brazil only in the sense of comparing slavery in the USA where a self-sustaining slave population was developed, while Brazil continued the importation of enslaved Africans. She integrated slavery in Brazil in her teaching to illustrate how the experiences of being enslaved would be different from one place to another; to help students understand how the institution developed in different places.

Like Teacher N in the USA, the educator from the Dominican Republic also taught slavery in Brazil for comparative purposes, and pointed out to students that the slavery system which existed in Brazil was closer to the system developed in Spanish-speaking America.

## Africans in Western Europe in the 18th Century

The educator in the Dominican Republic taught that the development of the new slavery system in America, and with it, the dehumanization of the African, changed the status of Africans in Europe at the same time. He described to his students the African presence in Europe at that time as 'doing some type of service task'. He pointed out, however, that not all Africans then were just servants and that some of them had been integrated into the system since the eighteenth century. Racism was not yet extant in western society so one could find people of African ancestry of high standing in most of the European countries, and especially in Italy and the Iberian Peninsula. He tried to find records to support this.

He also told his students about King Christophe of Haiti who sent Africans to Paris and Rome to study and that they were admitted to the best universities at the beginning of the nineteenth century. This happened, he said, because, even though the dehumanization process had been going on all along, it was not yet set as a racist system in the mentality of western society.

In the English-speaking Caribbean, the CXC history syllabus did not focus on the presence of Africans in Western Europe in the eighteenth century but rather on their presence in the Caribbean. Consequently, in Barbados and Jamaica, not a great deal was done on this theme. Teacher I (ii) in Barbados explained that the only possibility of addressing this theme occurred when teaching abolition and the conditions of enslaved Africans in England.

The teachers interviewed in the USA did not teach this theme.

## THE TRIANGULAR TRADE

Teachers in Barbados, Brazil and the USA all taught the triangular trade.

Teacher N in the USA taught the movement of goods and the effect that it had on the people who traded for these goods. She discussed the impact of the influx of European goods on African culture and similarly the impact of European goods coming into the Americas on American culture. Teacher I (ii) in Barbados employed a similar approach though her focus was the impact of the triangular trade on the West Indies.

In Brazil, in addition to the trade in enslaved Africans Teacher Q (i) emphasized the triangular trade in alcohol and sugar.

Teacher R in the USA taught the triangular trade to help students understand that the TTEA was what made the USA a wealthy country, that this did not happen by accident, nor by chance. She explained that this approach was taken to enable students to understand the economics of the trade because at their age — middle school students — it is difficult for them to comprehend why, if the system was so awful, people would do this to other people. She and her colleagues did not spend a great deal of time on the triangular trade outside of trying to communicate this understanding to their students.

## THE ROLE OF EUROPEAN COUNTRIES IN THE TRANSATLANTIC TRADE IN ENSLAVED AFRICANS

For Teacher I (iii) in Barbados, the European dimension came into focus when teaching how the TTEA was organized in Africa and she dealt with slave trading stations, trading companies and private traders. She also focused on Europe when teaching abolition.

Teacher I (iii) in examining the slave laws, looked at the approach of the French as opposed to the approach of the English and Spanish. She explained that there was not a specific topic on the role of the

Europeans in the trade, but that the theme was infused into the curriculum, especially when a comparative approach was taken as to what different countries did.

The Jamaican teachers adopted what seemed to be a more in-depth treatment of the role of European countries. They looked at Europe as a whole, but also at individual countries such as England, Spain and France which were more directly engaged in the trade since they had colonies in the Caribbean.

They felt it was always important to look at Portugal, as it was the first European country to take enslaved Africans from Africa to the Caribbean. Emphasis was also placed on the fact that Spain did not hold any fort in Africa; that they only brought enslaved Africans to the Caribbean. Spain never took out a slave ship from Africa to the Caribbean. Spain just stayed in the Caribbean and bought slaves from the others such as Portugal, England and France. They taught about the 'world power' (presumably Britain) and that the trade was a lucrative business for it; that European nations became wealthy through this venture. The teachers in Jamaica had less information on Denmark and Norway and more on Spain, England and France.

Teacher R in the USA emphasized Great Britain as being one of the first countries to end slavery and only 'touched' on the role of Portugal. She did not teach the involvement of France, Holland, Denmark and Norway but focused on what she referred to as 'the big ones'. Teacher S in the USA looked at the roles of the Portuguese, the Spanish, the French; the shifts in their involvement and the reasons for these shifts. For example, she discussed the reasons the English became involved in the trade and correlated that with the cultivation of sugar in the Caribbean. She linked this to the spread of the plantation from the Mediterranean to the islands off the coast of Africa and to the Caribbean and then up to America, providing her students with a sense of the plantation system moving across the Atlantic World, with sugar at the heart of it.

The educator in the Dominican Republic did not use this theme in his teaching. His students did not know much about the role of the British. From his perspective, the British have been very good at selling themselves as being the anti-slavery group, so he focused on the role of the port; specifically Liverpool as the richest port in the trade. He emphasized that he tried not to talk about Europe even though Europeans benefited the most from the trade. He resisted moral judgement on Europe as he felt the facts about Europeans were 'over played' in the Western world. He described himself as Afrocentric. As such, in dealing with the involvement of Africans in the TTEA, he presented the trade as an economic system. He discussed with students 'what was going on in Africa and the role of the African ... in the slave trade'. He noted that while some Africans were very open and appeared willing to discuss this issue, they really did not want to talk about it. While not trying to justify that period in Africa, at the same time he tried not to sanitize it. He looked at the facts: there were people who were benefiting from the trade and there were people who were hurt by it. He looked at Africa's involvement with the capitalist world, and how that in a way forced them, because it forced everybody, to participate in it. He did not place blame on either the Africans or the Europeans but merely tried to get his students to understand who benefited from the trade and who suffered as a result of it.

## MAJOR SLAVE TRADING PORTS

Teacher S in the USA taught the major slave trading ports in that country but not in Europe. The Brazilian teachers taught the ports of London, Seville and the city of Porto in Portugal.

## THE DURATION OF THE TRANSATLANTIC TRADE IN ENSLAVED AFRICANS

Teacher R in the USA taught her students that slavery always existed; that it was going on long before the USA was even a country. She located the commencement of the TTEA at around the 1200s and its cessation between the1700s and 1800s.

Teacher S in the USA located the official end of the trade in the USA in 1808. Some of her students were amazed at how long the trade lasted in other parts of the world, such as the Caribbean and Brazil, and at the idea that it extended into the 1880s. She placed the end of the TTEA outside of the USA around the 1870s.

When Teacher T (i) in Trinidad and Tobago questioned his students about the end of the TTEA, they thought that it varied between 1834 and 1838. He noted, however, that slavery continued in other parts of the world long after that, but that the TTEA lasted 400 years and many would say even longer than that. He preferred not to emphasize a period but tried to look at the phenomenon as an aspect of human history; a time when people only viewed each other as commodities. He did not accept the official dates for the end of the TTEA as the end of slavery and spoke of the reaction of one of his students when he used Saudi Arabia as an example. In his class of different religious persuasions he had the experience of discussing an article from *Newsweek* magazine dealing with slavery which illustrated that slavery was still prevalent in some countries such as Mauritania, India and Saudi Arabia in modern times. He recalled that one student of Islamic background became annoyed at the mention of Saudi Arabia, even though he drew from documentary evidence. His intention, he explained, was to show that although the TTEA may have ended in the nineteenth century, enslaved persons are still being traded up to today; that human beings see each other as commodities. He pointed out to his students the fact that if there is an economic desire for something the economy will find a way to serve that desire. He also spoke to them about the kinds of dreams people in Trinidad and Tobago harbour as they grow up: to build a big house and have 'one or two maids'. People still have these ideas so he tries to make these linkages. He also pointed out to his students that although they may believe that drug pushing is wrong and evil, many of their own relatives were involved in it. That in the same way that the drug pusher was not looking at the lives that he or she was destroying likewise the enslaver was just looking at the profit. Once there was profit the trade continued.

Brazilian teachers taught their students that the TTEA lasted three and a half centuries.

Teacher J (iii) in Jamaica taught her students the trade started in the late 1400s. In general, though, teachers in Jamaica and Barbados discussed when the trade started and ended in specific European countries.

## How Enslaved Africans were Shipped and The Middle Passage

Teacher I (iv) in Barbados spent a great deal of time on these themes. The educator in the Dominican Republic explained he presented this theme 'as the normal history would present it.' He tried to find out about the role of his African ancestors in the trade since, he explained, Africans were not only shipped, but took part in the shipment of their own brothers and sisters. No attempt was made to blame anyone. He examined the conditions of the enslaved people on these ships. He mentioned that, in the Dominican Republic, Places of Memory exist which can support the teaching of this theme.

Teachers R and S in the USA said it was important that their students understand the nature of the Middle Passage. They discussed how the trade altered the swimming habits of sharks because they would follow the slave ships to feed on the bodies being dumped off. The content knowledge they provided of the Middle Passage communicated to their students the terrible experience of this voyage and Teacher R elaborated they wanted their students to understand how human cargo was transported and that it was an awful experience. This was a major part of their curriculum. From visiting scholars students would learn how long the voyage took, how horrific it was and the stress of the people who survived it.

The theme of the Middle Passage was not discussed with the teachers from the English-speaking Caribbean since this researcher was already aware that they taught the Middle Passage. However, there was some discussion of the Middle Passage with these teachers under the thematic area (ix) 'How Enslaved Africans were shipped' and at other points during the interview sessions, such as the emotional dimension of students' responses to the TTEA discussed in Chapter 6.

## The Number of Enslaved Africans a Typical Slave Ship Crossing the Atlantic Carried

Several teachers, in discussing this theme tended to speak of total numbers of enslaved Africans transported during the TTEA, rather than numbers transported by a typical slave ship.

Teacher S in the USA mentioned that a visiting scholar provided some information about the numbers of enslaved Africans typically transported on a slave ship. This scholar explained that if the boat's maximum capacity was 600 they would pack maybe 900 people in because they knew they were likely to lose some of the cargo and also, if they ran out of food or water, they would just dump the sickest and the oldest ones. She wanted to convey that it was a question of economics and that people, just out of sheer greed, would put human beings in that situation.

Teacher N in the USA gave an estimate of four to five hundred enslaved persons being transported in a typical slave ship but admitted that this was not something she knew a great deal about. She used the David Eltis database, looked at the length of the Middle Passage and wondered about the ship building industry and the size of the ships built for the purpose of the trade. She did not realize that by the 1800s slave ships were getting smaller but seemed faster. Her students kept thinking about the fact that ships were actually built for the purpose of transporting enslaved Africans.

Teacher Q (iv) in Brazil used numbers such as 600 or 300 slaves 'but always two or three times the capacity of the ship.' He would point out to his students that the mortality rate was high. Around 40 per cent of the enslaved Africans being transported might die during the journey. At a point, the slave ship was called a *tumbeiro*, a tomb.

Barbadian teachers expressed the view that it was not possible to give any particular figure. Like the teachers from Jamaica, they made the point that the slave ship was always packed beyond capacity, with overcrowded ships carrying up to 700 enslaved Africans. This was the point they emphasized in their teaching. The teachers from Jamaica used the analogy of a tin of sardines to communicate to their students the overcrowding of slave ships and discussed the resulting mortality rates.

## Maroons

In 2001, students of Teacher S in the USA participated in a stage production about the Maroon community. Teacher R explained that there were several Maroon communities in the New Orleans area because of its geography, and that enslaved Africans who ran away were able to hide and survive in the swamps. There was a supply of water and food there, so the Maroon communities developed. Some residents were aware of their Maroon ancestry and were able to trace their heritage back to a freed man for more than a century.

Teacher Q (i) in Brazil organized field trips to communities called *quilombos* where runaway slaves would seek refuge. Mention was also made of *capoeira*, a dance which the enslaved Africans 'transformed into a powerful weapon against domination by the slave owners.' He indicated that in the state of Maranhao in North Eastern Brazil there was still one such community, so he took his students to the village to talk to these people who are the direct descendants of the enslaved Africans who ran away. He explained that the economy, social life and culture of the *quilombo,* described as trêchão, was still based on the concept of community. The land was owned by all. The harvest of crops was divided equally among everyone. In another community, Pará, they noted the intrusion of external culture into the *quilombo*. The teacher lamented the consequent weakening of their cultural identity evident in the replacement of images of the leaders who fought for them, such as Zombi, by other images.

A parallel can be drawn between the interests of the American and Brazilian teachers who seemed to share a common focus on contemporary manifestations of Maroon settlements. On the theme of resistance by the enslaved, Brazilian teachers also spoke of a specific case of enslaved Muslims in an area called Malizes, who came from North West Africa. It was explained that, 'they staged a revolt in Bahia in 1831 which lasted for a few hours – the Malizes revolt.'

Barbadian teachers taught their students about Maroons, even though, they explained, this was not a theme they could emphasize in the case of Barbados because of its geography. Jamaica was highlighted instead. This would seem to indicate that in Barbados, the identification and naming of national heroes such as Bussa who led a rebellion in 1816 notwithstanding, the curriculum still had some way to go in reflecting the contributions of such national heroes who had to resort to *marronage*. However, the Barbadian teachers pointed out to their students that the enslaved people in Barbados had their own ways of resisting such as 'malingering' or poisoning slave owners. It was important to highlight this as some students tended to think that the enslaved Africans in Barbados were passive.

The Jamaican teachers stressed the importance of the Maroon communities as a 'refuge for slaves to runaway' and seek protection. They referred to the existence of a Maroon settlement in Scots Hall, Jamaica and they usually invited a representative of that settlement to come in and mount a display for students. Mention was made of the fact that, in Jamaica, there were heritage week celebrations and Maroon history was a very important part of the celebrations.

The educator in the Dominican Republic discussed with his students Maroon women in Brazil from a comparative perspective. He compared Maroon women in Brazil with Maroon women in 'the islands' and also talked about the fact that they were connected, that is, Maroon communities in different islands had links with one another.

## TOUSSAINT L'OUVERTURE

Teacher N in the USA indicated that she did not teach Toussaint L'Ouverture as much as she should. She had done her undergraduate thesis on the 'slave islands' of South Carolina and 'the coming of freedom to the slave islands.' In 1861, early in the Civil War, the North came in and freed the slaves and in her thesis she focused on what the freed slaves were being taught 'in terms of defining freedom.' She was intrigued by the fact that Toussaint was being used as a symbol of freedom among the freed slaves; that his picture was being hung in the cabins of formerly enslaved people, although at the time she did not fully appreciate the significance of this for them. She was now planning to incorporate in her teaching what Toussaint L'Ouverture and the rebellion he led represented for those who were formerly enslaved in the USA.

The Barbadian teachers, in teaching this theme looked at: (i) the independence of Haiti; (ii) Toussaint as a black teacher and a hero; (iii) those who came after Toussaint; (iv) the Haitian Revolution; and (v) resistance. The Jamaican teachers, in teaching the Haitian Revolution, had to teach Toussaint L'Ouverture. The same was true of the teachers in Trinidad and Tobago.

Teacher T (ii) in Trinidad and Tobago said that Toussaint

L'Ouverture was covered in the history syllabus of the Caribbean Examinations Council (CXC) and also in the Cambridge Advanced Level West Indian paper which was now called Caribbean History. She explained that teachers had to focus on emancipation in the French West Indies and the specific content area is Haiti, so they teach the Haitian Revolution, the forces that precipitated it, the role of Toussaint and after Toussaint, the leaders that followed: Dessalines, Boyer, Christophe. This topic was being done in great detail at the Sixth Form level.

Teacher T (i) in Trinidad and Tobago taught Haiti and Toussaint from two different perspectives as, he said, there was the temptation to see Toussaint only in a heroic light. He introduced his students to new evidence that the higher proportion of new arrivals from Africa, in comparison with the enslaved Creoles, may have 'brought from Africa ideas of the running of the state' and this may have also been a factor in the rebellion. He taught that enslaved Africans coming from the Congo region may have come to Haiti with their ideas about the rights of the king and that these might have been factors leading to the rebellion. He deals with the fact that the Haitian Revolution is also seen as a by-product of the French Revolution owing to the weaknesses it created in the colony. He emphasized that the Haitian Revolution was not started by Toussaint; that it may have been, to some extent, some sort of opportunism on his part. In his teaching he adopted what he referred to as 'the C.L.R. James position' that Toussaint used his opportunities for the purpose of liberating a people rather than for his own personal advancement.

## WHY THE TRANSATLANTIC TRADE IN ENSLAVED AFRICANS TO THE CARIBBEAN WAS STOPPED

Teacher Q (i), in Brazil, highlighted the existence of various plans for abolition. There was the plan of the elite class, the popular plan of armed resistance, and the parliamentary or official plan. The elite steered their plan through parliamentary avenues. There were several armed groups involved in the popular plan called *caifazes*. It was the parliamentary plan that was successful. In Brazil, the process was slow, gradual. First, the abolition of the trade, then slowly, slavery itself. There were the laws like the sexagenarian law. Each of the laws defined a right to which blacks would be entitled. The free womb law stated that any slave born after that date would be free. Under the sexagenarian law, slaves over the age of 60 were declared free.

Teacher Q (ii) added that they also taught students that, at a given moment in history, the ruling class realized that slavery was not bringing in the necessary profits. It was becoming very onerous to pay, in terms of food, for slave labour. Many were dying. They believed that freeing the enslaved Africans and Creoles would cause prices of commodities to fall. There was, therefore, an all out mobilization to this end.

Teacher Q (iii) continued that they placed in context the consolidation of capitalism and pressure from England to end both trafficking in enslaved Africans and slavery. They also had to factor in immigration: the Spaniards, the Germans and Italians coming in to replace the slave labour force. With abolition, enslaved Africans were not considered to be essential to the economy and their places were taken by the immigrants. It was easier for the immigrant to work because he or she represented qualified labour. The slave owners did not provide for the education of the enslaved because it was expensive and they were no longer seen as important.

Teacher N in the USA planned to address this theme in the future by putting the abolitionist movement in the USA into a global perspective. She did not deal with the story of the abolitionist movement until she got in her US history class to the area just before the Civil War. She planned to deal with the rise of abolition in different parts of the world and then try to get a sense of where the USA fit into that bigger picture.

Teacher I (i) in Barbados explained that she always emphasized that the trade was stopped for economic reasons, while acknowledging that there were abolitionists who also worked to stop it. In recent times, the teaching of this theme had been refocused to examine not just the humanitarianism of some Europeans who had very good and genuine intentions but also the actions of the enslaved Africans who contributed to the cessation of the trade. She referred, in particular, to the Bussa rebellion in Barbados which was one of the events that alerted the countries participating in the trade that they could not be comfortable in a slave society as before. This focus on the Bussa rebellion was a recent one whereas, in the past, the focus would have been mainly on the European humanitarians. Recent literature has helped teachers to refocus and they were seeing that a number of things happened to contribute to the abolition of slavery.

Teachers in Jamaica also focused on economic reasons for the end of the trade. However, they promoted an 'objective' approach to the study of this theme, pointing out to students the involvement of white people in England who were trying to abolish the trade. Teacher J (ii) explained that it was necessary to do so because the students become very 'sensitive' when this topic is being taught and most of them feel that 'the white person... didn't have anything to do with the stopping of the trade.' Teachers need, therefore, to emphasize that even though whites enslaved Africans, others in England were trying to abolish the trade.

## THE HUMAN TRAGEDY OF THE TRANSATLANTIC TRADE IN ENSLAVED AFRICANS

Teacher I (i) in Barbados explained that her students were 'confounded' by the fact that the Africans outnumbered the Europeans in Africa and in the Caribbean 'and yet they did not rise up and take over and resist this situation.' Sometimes, as teachers, they had difficulty explaining this and could only offer the explanation that 'the Europeans had superior weapons.' Still, the students would continue to pose questions about the situation and tended to view the Africans as being 'either weak or stupid'. Teachers then highlighted the human tragedy of enslavement, that they might have had to become slave drivers, and be obliged to flog their own relatives or somebody who was a friend or, if they were not in such a position, they might have been the ones flogged. The human tragedy of the trade was also explored in terms of its impact on the African continent and its legacies which remain with us today. She stated that in discussing the human tragedy of the trade on the African continent they tend to examine issues such as the destruction of families; fear of capture; and then they sometimes consider the modern day situation and the legacies of the trade. Some of these legacies are evident in how we treat each other, in terms of physical characteristics, in terms of social mobility. The continuing human tragedy of the trade manifests itself in the form of mental slavery. She stressed that this is still to be addressed.

Teachers T (i) and T (v) in Trinidad and Tobago had different emphases in dealing with the human tragedy of the trade. While Teacher T (v) adopted a somewhat factual approach, Teacher T (i) focused on more philosophical issues, centred on the hopelessness which confronted the enslaved Africans, the legacy of negativity which continues to pursue people of African descent and the negative impact of the trade on the human development of people of African ancestry. When reading and teaching the TTEA Teacher T (i) was struck by the fact that a significant section of humanity had no avenue of any sort of social mobility or improvement in their lot, because they were condemned from birth till death. An entire section of mankind was condemned to a life of servitude, death, exploitation, did not have the advantage of developing with its full potential for such an extended period of time. Many people have attempted to gloss over these issues, giving the impression that the Transatlantic Trade in Enslaved Africans was not a phenomenon in world history because other groups of people in history have also suffered victimization and exploitation. The TTEA, however, was a phenomenon since Africans were discriminated against on the basis of race. With the development of the trade, it was necessary for the Europeans to see the African as something negative, as sub-human, in order to justify their own evil. That legacy has stayed with us even today. The trade has left us, up to today, with an overriding belief that some people are still more important than others, and this is extremely painful and is one of the damages that it has wrought, he stressed.

The educator in the Dominican Republic also commented on the negative impact of the trade on human development. He stated that the dehumanization of a group of people was more than a tragedy and that, in teaching this theme, he put emotion into his treatment of the subject. Dehumanizing a person is a long process and regaining one's humanity is another long, long process and this is now the important issue. In adopting an Afrocentric approach to the subject, therefore, his focus was on the strength of the enslaved Africans.

# AFRICA: Benin, Senegal, the Gambia

## Supply of enslaved Africans to the New World

Teacher H in the Gambia was of the view that, 'It is very important for the students to know where the slaves came from.' She focused on the organization of the trade, on the process which took place in Africa at the time and the scale of the trade in terms of the numbers of enslaved people involved. Implicit in her account was the recognition of the involvement of Africans in the supply of enslaved Africans. She explained to her students that slave traders negotiated with African slave dealers on the coast for the purchase of slaves. The Europeans did not go into the interior themselves. She emphasized that the supply came from the interior because the coastal regions were not very populated.

Teacher F in Senegal first looked at the manner in which the Africans were captured. This presented an opportunity to discuss slavery in Africa since, he explained, that also existed. He examined how an individual became a slave in Africa and then looked at how individuals were captured and sold to the Europeans. He explained that there were several ways in which one could become a slave in Africa. A prisoner of war might become a slave or slavery might be punishment for a crime. There were also instances of force involving kidnap and enslavement. He said the TTEA led people to search for enslaved Africans, to see them as a means of income. Often the Europeans forced Africans to sell other Africans into slavery; the superior weaponry of the Europeans made this possible.

Teacher G in Benin elaborated on the question of slavery in Africa. He explained that if people were unable to repay a debt they gave their own children as slaves to compensate. He said this practice continues to be a problem in Nigeria even today.

## How enslaved Africans were used

Teacher H in the Gambia taught that the Atlantic Slave Trade started because of the discovery of the Americas. The New World needed a strong labour force on the plantations and for mining. The indigenous peoples found in the New World were not considered strong enough for the task and Europeans could not survive the climatic conditions.

The teachers from Benin and Senegal distinguished between the uses made of enslaved Africans in Africa and in the Americas. They taught that in Africa the enslaved Africans acted as house slaves, servants to royal families, field workers, and as eunuchs in the service of the king's wives. In the Americas, they were used as labour on plantations to build the European economy, and for sexual purposes – more of a by-product than a main cause. They told their students that those who were taken to America by the Europeans were used for the development of agriculture in the New World. Their labour was necessary for the development of the plantations: sugar cane, tobacco, coffee, and all the products that fuelled the economy in Europe. They also looked at their work conditions in the field.

The teacher from Senegal elaborated on the nature of the distinctions that were made when teaching students the use of enslaved Africans in Africa as opposed to in the Americas. He explained that those who were not sold at all were assigned to families. They accepted their service conditions because they were well treated. Their work conditions were not as harsh as those endured by those of the transatlantic trade. These enslaved Africans were considered part of the family and in some instances they even occupied very important positions in society. They had a voice; they were free to express themselves. The king had confidence in these slaves; he knew that they would not betray him. The eunuchs were at the wives' disposal to go out and to do difficult chores. Since they were usually castrated they could not have sexual relations with any of the wives. Their role was to guard the harem. They were there to monitor or even to spy on the wives.

The sexual abuse of enslaved Africans occurred both in Africa and in the Americas. The white slave traders would enter the slave dungeon, *l'esclaverie*, select the loveliest girls and sexually abuse them. This is responsible for the mulatto society in Senegal, in Gorée and St Louis.

## SLAVERY IN BRAZIL

Teacher F in Senegal mentioned slavery in Brazil in discussing the places from which the enslaved Africans left and the ports at which they arrived and this included Brazil. Teacher G in Benin added that through the study of Brazil the cultural impact of the TTEA was discussed. An average of 40 per cent of enslaved Africans went to Brazil; a significant issue when teaching the cultural impact of the Trade. He looked at the consequences of the African presence in Brazil, for example, the music, dances and religion.

## AFRICANS IN WESTERN EUROPE IN THE EIGHTEENTH CENTURY

Teacher H in the Gambia taught that the TTEA started some time around the mid-fifteenth century. By the eighteenth century it was at its peak and presence of Africans in Western Europe at that time could not be over-emphasized.

## THE TRIANGULAR TRADE

Teacher F in Senegal referred to the treatment of this theme as inevitable.

## THE ROLE OF EUROPEAN COUNTRIES IN THE TRADE IN ENSLAVED AFRICANS

This was not an area of emphasis for Teacher H in the Gambia, although she did examine Britain in detail. Teacher G in Benin mentioned Portugal and Spain. While previously he would not have treated with Norway, he now did so, 'because of UNESCO's objective to shed light on all areas of the problem.'

## MAJOR SLAVE TRADING PORTS

Teacher H in the Gambia did not cover slave-trading ports as a specific thematic area. She wondered whether this represented an inadequacy in her teaching. She tended to focus on those thematic areas that were to be examined, but indicated that she wanted to know more about the slave trading ports.

Teacher F in Senegal said he and his colleagues taught practically 'all the slave trading ports'. When he taught the origins of the European slave ships, he mentioned the relevant ports. He also taught the Spanish ports which he considered to be the most important, and the maritime power of the Portuguese and the Turks.

Teacher G in Benin taught his students about the ports of Nantes, Liverpool, Bristol and Lisbon.

## THE DURATION OF THE SLAVE TRADE

Teacher F in Senegal insisted on the fact that, after the TTEA was abolished, a clandestine trade ensued, and referred to modern day slavery. He explained that in the recent past, he and his colleagues visited a village to conduct a survey among the villagers. They were talking to the villagers about the royalty that existed there when an elderly man told them that the French had dethroned the last king in his village because he was caught selling enslaved Africans to the English slave traders. This happened in a zone near The Gambia. He shared this information to support the point that even after the trade was abolished there were Africans who still covertly engaged in the trade. This was after the colonial conquest – the 1800s, 1890 or thereabout. Even up to today, he elaborated, slavery continues as seen in the reported cases of the boat of children sold in Gabon and the Ivory Coast and people being kidnapped around the area of Lake Chad. Teacher G in Benin taught that the trade lasted 'four centuries or even more than four centuries'; that it started in the sixteenth century and went up to the nineteenth century.

## HOW ENSLAVED AFRICANS WERE SHIPPED AND THE MIDDLE PASSAGE

Teacher H in the Gambia explained to students the organization of the trade in three different stages and its triangular dimensions; she would tell them that, at that time, the ships were neither very big nor were they modern.

She also discussed the goods the Europeans brought with them when they came to the Guinea Coast and that on the return journey, enslaved Africans would replace these goods on the ships.

Teacher G in Benin dealt with the journey across the Atlantic and, as a point of departure, examined with students the placement of the enslaved Africans on the ships, using film and materials provided by UNESCO. He highlighted the conditions under which the enslaved Africans were shipped pointing out, for example, the size of the boat and the number of levels of the boat which gave the students an idea of the enormity of the trade and that the enslaved Africans were treated as mere commodities. He also discussed revolts by enslaved Africans that took place on board the ships. For example, some threw themselves into the sea. The sick, the dying, they were thrown into the sea. He taught about the horrible conditions that existed.

Teacher H in the Gambia located the Middle Passage within the organization of the trade. She explained that the Middle Passage was the journey from Africa across the Atlantic to the New World and provided students with a description of the slavers and the enslaved Africans during this stage of the journey. In dealing with this theme she focused on the enslaved Africans whereas in dealing with other stages of the trade, such as the first stage – capture – the focus would be on the Europeans going out to Africa.

## THE NUMBER OF ENSLAVED AFRICANS A TYPICAL SLAVE SHIP CROSSING THE ATLANTIC CARRIED

Teachers G and F, from Benin and Senegal respectively found it difficult to try to give their students numbers, given that there was always controversy surrounding this issue. However, they made the following points:

(i) Based on the different sources consulted, the figures had to be high so that the traders could make a good profit. For traders to have maximum profits they had to overcrowd the ship, especially when the number of enslaved Africans lost during the journey was considered.
(ii) They considered the capacity of ships.
(iii) While they estimated about 20 million to have been transported for the duration of the trade, simply quoting figures lacked authenticity.
(iv) They considered mortality on board and losses at other stages of the trade from capture to arrival in the Americas.

Teacher G in Benin drew attention to the need for accuracy. He did not like quoting figures as they could not be convincing. He explained it was important to consider the ship captain's needs and what he could have accommodated and estimated that the typical slave ship would carry about 150 to 200 enslaved Africans. He pointed out to students that to have an exact idea of the number of Africans reduced to slavery — from their origins in Africa to the arrival in the USA — they had to consider the losses. For each enslaved African that was sold in America, six died. Some died during the village raid, some during the transfer to the coast, and the ones who died during the journey, including those who revolted.

Teacher H in the Gambia did not discuss actual numbers either because she had not been able 'to hold on to figures'. Rather, she explained the kind of thinking which would have informed how slave dealers would pack their ships in the interest of making a high profit. She told them the slave dealers were business people and sometimes the ships were not too big so that they tried to be very cost effective and took as many enslaved Africans as they could. The number of enslaved Africans that could be shipped conveniently by two voyages was normally packed into one voyage to save costs. She described enslaved Africans as being packed like sardines in a tin.

## Maroons

Teacher G in Benin said that it was now compulsory to teach students the rebellions organized by the enslaved. This was done to demonstrate to students that, among the enslaved, there were those who did not accept their fate. Rather, they fled to the bushes where they organized rebellions. This form of resistance, *marronage*, he said, was developed in the Caribbean and America.

Teacher F in Senegal pointed to successful rebellions. He pointed out that when they were captured, enslaved Africans showed resistance during the journey and upon arrival to the USA or the Caribbean, they continued to resist. They did not resign themselves to their fate. Whenever they had an opportunity to resist, they did so. He also discussed with students those rebellions that were quite successful, for example, the 'railroad rebellion' that took place in the USA.

Teacher H in the Gambia taught Maroons under the themes of the abolition of the slave trade and the effects of the trade on Africa, such as the founding of Sierra Leone and Liberia. She explained that the Maroons were among the groups of people to arrive in Sierra Leone in 1898 as a result of the abolition of the TTEA.

## TOUSSAINT L'OUVERTURE

Teacher F in Senegal talked about Toussaint L'Ouverture when he was on the subject of Haiti, the Haitian Revolution and the independence of Haiti. Teacher G in Benin, in addition, taught L'Ouverture's origins in Benin and his death. A statue of Toussaint, recently erected at *L'Ada* in Benin, is used as a resource in this regard. He takes his students to see the statue. He also touches on Dessalines.

## WHY THE SLAVE TRADE TO THE CARIBBEAN WAS STOPPED

Teacher H in the Gambia looked at both the humanitarian and economic arguments for the end of the trade. With regard to humanitarian reasons she and her colleagues discussed with students religious bodies, the French philosophers, the Greek humanitarians, and the enslaved people themselves. On the question of economic reasons for the cessation of the trade, they talked about the Industrial Revolution and informed students about the controversy among historians today as to why the trade was stopped. Some historians argue that the humanitarian reasons were more important, while others argue that the economic were far more important, or that neither reason alone provides an adequate explanation but that it was really a combination of the two.

Her personal position was that the economic reasons were more important, because the humanitarian lobby had been going on since the initiative of the Quakers who were the ones who first raised their voices against the trade in the seventeenth century and nothing was done. Other religious bodies raised their voices and still nothing was done. The British spearheaded abolition when they realized they no longer needed slave labour because the transition from an agricultural economy to an industrial economy was taking place and those with vested interests in the trade started to experience losses.

This provided the opening for the humanitarians to break through.

In teaching this theme, Teacher G in Benin taught that from the eighteenth century, there was an economic re-conversion because of the Industrial Revolution. Machinery replaced human labour and consequently 'there was a cutback on the slave trade'. In this theme he treated the USA and the Caribbean in a general way. Teacher F in Senegal also dealt with rebellion, in particular the Santo Domingo revolution, the abolition of the trade and finally, the independence of Haiti.

## The human tragedy of the TTEA

In treating with the human tragedy of the TTEA, Teachers G and H in Benin and the Gambia respectively, focused on the effects of the trade on the population of Africa. Teacher G showed his students the decline in the population of Africa and the loss of manpower to Africa, brought about by the trade. He pointed out to students that during the seventeenth century, the African continent had approximately the same population size that China has today. Today, comparisons between the two countries reveal a gap. The gap is seen as proof that the trade stole a great deal of manpower from Africa. Africans consider this to be one of the reasons for the underdevelopment of Africa today.

For Teachers G in Benin and F in Senegal, the human tragedy of the trade was communicated to their students from the onset and included capture and the conditions into which the enslaved Africans were taken. Visits to Places of Memory were used to underscore the human tragedy of the trade and the loss of identity and dignity that came with such a fate.

Teacher G in Benin emphasized the enormity and duration of the trade. When they compare the atrocities committed during slavery with those of the both world wars, the cruelties of slavery seem much higher than both wars put together. They teach about the human tragedy of the trade especially at school outings, when they visit the various Places of Memory such as Ouidah, and 'The Gate of No Return' where they can imagine the state of mind of enslaved Africans before they were taken away from their native land. He talked about 'The Tree of Forgetting'. Before setting sail, the women went around this tree seven times and the men nine times as a symbol of their leaving behind everything they cherished.

Teacher H in the Gambia discussed the destruction and underdevelopment of Africa; the weakening of the culture; and loss of initiative representative of the human tragedy of the trade on the continent of Africa. She stated that when they talk about the effects of the trade on Africa, they talk about the tremendous loss of life and property in Africa, the destruction of the population of Africa, the horrors of the trade, the treatment of its victims. They also discuss the ways in which it contributed to the underdevelopment of Africa; it disrupted culture in Africa. The strong, the virile were taken away and only the feeble were left. It created an atmosphere of anarchy or insecurity in which people could not engage in meaningful social activities. It killed initiative in Africa, like the progress of indigenous industries. This loss of skill and potential development has left today's Africa dependent on the West. With the advent of the TTEA the local workers and others abandoned their skills in favour of the more lucrative business of the trade.

## EUROPE: ENGLAND, DENMARK

### SUPPLY OF ENSLAVED AFRICANS TO THE NEW WORLD

Teacher B in the UK indicated that an effort was made to present this theme in such a way that his students did not link slavery only with African cultures, but also with many countries in Europe. His was a very broad approach to the history of slavery in world civilization. He used the opportunity provided by the UNESCO project to reach out to other European schools to get case-study material about their countries' involvement in the TTEA.

Teacher A in the UK taught 'predominantly about slavery coming from West Africa.'

Teacher E in Denmark explored the numbers of enslaved persons who were taken from Africa with a specific interest in their destinations. This stands in contrast to a teacher in Barbados whose greater interest was in tribal origins.

## How Enslaved Africans Were Used

Teacher B in the UK looked at plantation life which was 'easier to resource from British textbooks because that theme is there all the way through; black people working on ships and in the British army; and black people in the Americas.' He tried to show the different roles of enslaved peoples over time. Teacher C in the UK explained, 'We study the types of jobs done by slaves on the plantations, the distribution of jobs by gender and the treatment of people according to their job or status as a slave.'

## Slavery in Brazil

Most of the teachers interviewed did not cover this topic. Teacher B in the UK said there was not 'time to cover all of those themes.'

Teacher E in Denmark said this theme was mentioned briefly. He said that, in relation to slavery, today's students think especially of the USA: the plantations in the South and the Civil War. They seem to understand there was slavery in the Caribbean but express surprise at its existence in Brazil.

## Africans in Western Europe in the Eighteenth Century

Teacher A in the UK traced the presence of Africans in Western Europe in the eighteenth century through the overall curriculum. For example, in dealing with the court of Henry VIII, she showed paintings depicting the courtiers, some of whom were black. She also looked at the presence of blacks in the UK from the year 1750 and in the 1900s. One of the personalities she discussed with students was Olaudah Equiano, who, as a child, was kidnapped into slavery and taken to the New World. He eventually bought his freedom and became involved in the anti-slavery movement in London. Teacher C in Hull also used Equiano as an example, though 'only slightly' to teach this theme.

The Danish teacher, Teacher E, normally taught from a Danish perspective and since there were 'very, very few Africans in Denmark at the time,' this theme was not addressed. The teachers interviewed in the USA did not teach this theme either.

Teacher B in Bristol taught students that Britain had always been multicultural; that black people in the eighteenth century in Bristol were not necessarily there as a result of slavery, though some were. He explained that there is a great deal of evidence of black people who came as domestic servants — such as Equiano — from ships or as sailors. He taught that black people were in London around the time of Elizabeth I, and tried to make sure that the black presence in Britain was established from as far back as possible and that throughout there was a positive image of blacks.

## THE TRIANGULAR TRADE

For Teacher A in the UK the TTEA was an important focus and its role in leading to Britain's industrialization and wealth was emphasized. This gives students the sense that this was not something that happened just in the Caribbean or Africa, but the part Britain played is vital and the goods that were being produced by the enslaved Africans fuelled the Industrial Revolution. For her, the idea of the development of trade leading to industrialization and riches is quite important. She wanted her students to understand that Britain's wealth was due to the exploitation of Africa.

For Teacher C in the UK the triangular trade was usually the point of departure, moving from the growth of industry in Britain to the need for places to trade manufactured goods.

## THE ROLE OF EUROPEAN COUNTRIES IN THE TTEA

Teacher A in the UK examined with her students how Britain's wealth was dependent on the cotton being produced in the Americas. She did not teach students about other countries that participated in the TTEA. Britain was also the focus of Teacher C in the UK, as part of a unit on Britain from 1750 to 1900.

On the other hand, Teacher B in the UK indicated that, given the demands of the national curriculum which focused on Europe, his school addressed the TTEA as a turning point for the prosperity of Europe. The trade was the venture capital for everything, for much of the Industrial Revolution, and it was paid for by somebody else's labour. In order to make that work and fit within the requirements of the UK's national curriculum they had to consider the impact of other European countries.

Teacher E in Denmark focused first on his own country and then on Britain. He explored this theme by looking at statistics indicating which countries were the major transporters of enslaved Africans and had colonies in the New World. His objective in doing so was to give his students an idea of which countries played a dominant role in the trade.

## Major slave trading ports

Teachers A and C in London and Hull respectively, taught the ports of London, Liverpool and Bristol. Teacher B in Bristol focused on Bristol and its wealth since Bristol was a 'big slaving port' where a minority prospered from the trade. They did not look at the rest of Europe.

Teacher B in Bristol tended to speak of what he and his colleagues would be able to teach in relation to thematic areas which they were not already teaching. He noted that they would be able to teach about Liverpool, London and Bristol and expressed the hope that, on the basis of contact with European colleagues, they would be able to learn a little bit more about major slave trading ports in Europe. He observed that few of his students had the opportunity or resources to travel and this presented possible difficulties. Nonetheless, he would try to make them aware of the nature of the involvement of small European nations in the trade.

Teacher E in Denmark taught only about Bristol and Liverpool in England and not about any other ports in mainland Europe. He noted that the TTEA was not as significant in Denmark as in other European countries.

## The duration of the slave trade

Teacher B in the UK presented the TTEA within the period of the 1400s to the 1800s and considered the long-term legacies. However, he and his colleagues established for students the concept of 'slave' as not just being black or African but rather, like Teacher R in the USA, presented the idea of slavery as a problem that has been around for a long time, as well as a 'multicultural concept of slavery'. He also spoke of the existence of several 'slave type relations' today and indicated that this question should be a very open-ended one.

Teacher A in the UK explained she and her colleagues taught students that the trade lasted hundreds of years, but she did not think they understood this at all. The time span was too great for them to grasp. Teacher E in Denmark explained to his students that the trade from Africa to Europe started in the fifteenth century; expanded to the New World in the sixteenth century, and continued into the nineteenth century.

## HOW ENSLAVED AFRICANS WERE SHIPPED AND THE MIDDLE PASSAGE

Teacher B in the UK, describing this theme as very interesting, said his pupils tried to understand the inhumanity of the slave traders through their treatment of the enslaved Africans.

Teacher A in the UK taught this theme in great detail and said his students developed a real sense of it. The Danish Teacher E taught the Middle Passage over a two-week period.

Teacher C in the UK looked at the conditions and food and explained tight and loose packing, noting that his students could not believe how little room the enslaved Africans had on board the slave ship. He also discussed death rates in different geographic regions. Teacher B in the UK described this theme as very easy to teach using British textbooks.

## THE NUMBER OF ENSLAVED AFRICANS A TYPICAL SLAVE SHIP CROSSING THE ATLANTIC CARRIED

Teacher A in the UK indicated that while she emphasized the magnitude and duration of the trade, she thought that it was beyond the grasp of her students. However, when the numbers were placed in the context that the Caribbean did not always have people of African origin, then they began to understand its impact.

Teacher B in the UK spoke of the impossibility of quantifying the number of enslaved Africans that the ships carried, of knowing how many people were kidnapped, enslaved, and moved around given the disagreement among historians on the numbers that were involved.

As a consequence, he explained, this did not constitute a major focus in his teaching. He spoke of the problems that teachers might face dealing with this aspect of the history of the trade if the difficulty with the precision of the quantitative aspects of the trade was what they themselves had been taught. Teachers could not, for example, estimate numbers of deaths and numbers of survivors.

Teacher E in Denmark did not discuss how many enslaved Africans would be on a typical slave ship, but rather, looked at different slavers, how many enslaved Africans they might hold and how they were stored. Nonetheless, Teacher E in Denmark did explain to his students that there are many different figures. Referring to the number of enslaved Africans transported during the trade as opposed to the number transported on a typical slave ship he indicated 'the figure that we usually say is twelve million slaves. Some would say five million, others eighteen million.'

## Maroons

Apart from Teacher A in the UK who did not teach her students about Maroons, this theme was generally taught. Teacher B in the UK dealt with the related theme of resistance since, as he explained, the 'classic British textbook ideal would be to look at people as passive.' Teacher C in the UK taught about Maroons only very minimally to mention what happened to enslaved persons who ran away. Texts in his school contained little about Maroons.

Teacher E in Denmark had not been familiar with the concept of Maroons until he did a 'minor project' on reggae and looked at the history of Jamaica and the Maroons in Jamaica. He originally believed that *marronage* occurred principally in the West Indies but later discovered that as long as there was slavery, there was *marronage* throughout the Americas and Caribbean.

## Toussaint L'Ouverture

Teacher B in the UK indicated that, at his school, they looked at some key personalities, recognizing that from 'Britain's point of view, it's going to be easy for us to engage with British anti-slavery.' For the future, they would try to pick out key individuals who campaigned against the TTEA, key people who resisted, who wrote and were involved in the intellectual debate regarding anti-slavery. He hoped that Toussaint would be among these. Teacher E in Denmark explained that while the name looked familiar, he had never dealt with Toussaint L'Ouverture.

## WHY THE SLAVE TRADE TO THE CARIBBEAN WAS STOPPED

Teacher B in the UK planned to use the work of some West Indian scholars who were 'Marxist writers' and who took the position that abolition had nothing to do with campaigning to free enslaved Africans but for economic reasons. Other reasons for the end of slavery would also be examined. Teacher C in the UK who lived in Hull treated this theme 'in a bit of depth' as Hull was the birthplace and the parliamentary seat of William Wilberforce. Teacher E in Denmark discussed the theme quite a bit in relation to the concept of human rights. The French Revolution was used to explain that 'it became an ideal to treat all people in the same way. That France had to, or rather, did, abolish slavery.' He also taught that after the French Revolution slavery was reintroduced, and discussed with students the different views about the reasons behind abolition: that it was a result of the lobbying of religious groups; that it had nothing to do with religion, but rather, 'It was abolished because business was bad and it was no longer profitable.'

## THE HUMAN TRAGEDY OF THE TRANSATLANTIC TRADE IN ENSLAVED AFRICANS

Teacher C in the UK explained that the TTEA, by definition, cannot be seen as anything but a human tragedy and to underscore this he stressed the numbers of enslaved Africans transported and the inhumanity of the trade. Teacher A in the UK found it very difficult to talk to her students about the human tragedy of the trade, because of its close association with their families. Her students found it hard to admit that this had happened. She noted that teaching about human tragedy was not easy.

Teacher E in Denmark described teaching the TTEA as 'a very delicate matter,' adding that it was too simple to just look at the human tragedy, as this prevented one from getting into some other interesting aspects of the trade. He advocated going beyond focusing on the suffering caused by the trade to examine what caused it and was quite critical of those who exploited its human tragedy dimension, using this as a weapon or an excuse for negative behaviour. He argued that the TTEA was indeed a huge tragedy but that there have been many tragedies in world history though very few, if any, have been as large as the TTEA. What was essential was to ask ourselves why things like this happen; what is it in human nature that makes such things possible and to question as well whether such events can take place today. Slavery, he said, still goes on all over the world. We talk about the genocide in World War II and say that there has not been anything like it since. However, this is not the case. It happened in Kosovo, in Rwanda, Burundi. It still happens all over the world. So we have to focus on trying to get behind all those terrible acts instead of just focusing on the suffering. We have to ask ourselves what can make this happen.

This Danish teacher recounted a personal experience while he was working in the USA. Among his students was a black boy who used to disrupt the class and one day he told him to go to the assistant principal's office. The boy asked the teacher if he was doing this to him because he was black. The teacher felt that this student used his blackness as a weapon. He used his past as a weapon for his behaviour now. He believed that he could behave in a particular way now because someone did something to his ancestors two or 300 years ago. While this is a valid perspective for reflection on these issues, one must nonetheless acknowledge that the legacies of slavery linger, possibly unrecognised and misunderstood.

CHAPTER 5

# Teachers' Organization Of Content Knowledge

Chapter 5 presents findings relating to the question: How do teachers organize content knowledge of the historiography of the TTEA? It discusses teaching strategies including those found to be most successful; resources employed; issues relating to resources; and teachers' greatest challenges in teaching the trade. While the focus is on teachers' organization of subject content knowledge, reference is also made to inputs and views of administrators where relevant.

## Radical Teachers

Referring to the constraints of the national curriculum, Teacher B in the UK explained that teachers interested in teaching the TTEA have 'tried to be more radical...' and to find ways of spending more time teaching the subject. He emphasized that in teaching the subject, teachers had to have a very strong European focus in order to conform to the requirements of the national curriculum. He described what he and his colleagues were attempting as 'quite a daring strategy'.

Administrator 1 in the UK said teachers were looking at ways of 'deconstructing'; looking at teaching through open eyes as Britain tends to glorify its role in history in any context.

## THEMES AND CONCEPTS

### Slavery as a Long Established Idea

Teacher B in the UK presented the concept of slavery 'as being a very long established idea [that] goes back to ancient civilization,' and the TTEA as a 'European turning point'. Since 2001, he and his colleagues decided that, given its magnitude and significance, the subject of the trade warranted a whole term's work.

### Celebrating Positive Contributions of Africans

Referring to a UNESCO Associated Schools sponsored Youth Forum on the TTEA held in Bristol in 2001, Administrator 1 in the UK explained that the activities facilitated a journey of discovery of the positive contributions of Africans that have been lost in history. After quite a lot of debate the Forum was called *Commemorate and Celebrate* to celebrate the positive contributions of the African diaspora.

### Focus on Africa and the Middle Passage

Teacher E in Denmark used the themes of slavery and slave transportation in 'the Triangular Slave Trade' with a focus on the Africa situation and the Middle Passage. He considered the subject of the trade important for many reasons and could be approached from various perspectives. These included emotional issues, new information, bringing new insights to students, as well as dealing with the industrialization of Europe and its accumulation of wealth. A teacher could also lead a discussion on slavery using the works of the philosophers in Europe during the Enlightenment.

### Communicating the Humanity of the Enslaved Africans

Administrator 2 in the USA, in providing an overview of the implementation of the Project in a New Orleans public school, explained that the first thing dealt with was 'nomenclaturing' as this related to the use of the concept of the 'enslaved African' as opposed to the African as 'slave'. Their intention was to disempower the enslaver and the first way to do that was by dealing with nomenclature that was more humane. Enslaved Africans were people who were kidnapped, brutalized, oppressed, and whose descendants are still oppressed. They do not talk about the master but rather about the enslaver. They were not always successful and children still used the term 'slaves'. Nonetheless, this strategy proved effective with some children. He recognized that it worked with some of the teachers who prior to their participation in the UNESCO Project, were probably talking about slaves and masters but had begun talking about the enslaved and the enslavers. They had become sensitized to the extent that they changed their nomenclature.

Teachers R and S reiterated the concern of Administrator 2 in the USA relating to nomenclaturing, emphasizing the need to make very clear that Africans were not slaves but enslaved. Teacher R focused on communicating to her students the humanity of the enslaved Africans. She thought this important for her students to fully appreciate what it took for the enslaved Africans to survive. She worked diligently on getting her students to grasp the concept that Africans were enslaved so that students would appreciate the suffering and the strength that it took to survive this experience and to have a thriving community of descendants of enslaved Africans on the North American continent.

## Overcoming Hardship

Teachers R and S in the USA also communicated to their students the hardship that children born into slavery experienced and how they overcame those hardships. This was done in an attempt to show that they too could overcome some of the obstacles in their community, such as living in poverty. Using the narratives of Sojourner Truth and Frederick Douglass, they linked the history of the TTEA with their students' current reality in their communities. This gave students a sense of ownership of their history.

## Valuing People of African Descent and Acts of Resistance

The Brazilian teachers first treated the theme of slavery in general, then the specific case of the Americas. They dealt with the need to value and not victimize people of African descent using the medium of black culture in Brazil.

Like the teachers in Barbados, those in Brazil integrated the concept of resistance in their teaching to respond to the traditional view of the African as passive. One of these teachers spoke of the necessity of dealing with the myth of passivity to show the resistance Africans put up against slavery: escapes, killings of overseers, formations of *quilombos,* suicides, abortions, and above all, religious syncretism which all work towards the deconstruction of the idea of passivity.

## Afrocentrism

Teacher T (iii) in Barbados and the educator in the Dominican Republic employed an Afrocentric approach to teaching the TTEA. The educator in the Dominican Republic defined his Afrocentric teaching as locating 'the thinking of the African at the centre of the history'. For example, when talking about the arrival of the Europeans in the Americas, he does not start with the arrival of Christopher Columbus; rather, he begins by describing what was going on in Africa and the rest of the world at the time. He begins with Africa at around 1492; this he described as an Afrocentric perspective.

## Involvement of Africans in the Transatlantic Trade in Enslaved Africans

In Jamaica, the involvement of Africans in the trade arose when teaching the origins of the enslaved Africans. Teacher J (i) said she always discussed West Africa, the forest states, the savannahs, how Africans were living before the Europeans interrupted their lives. This was done so that students would understand that it was not the white person who actually started slavery in Africa; that slavery existed in Africa and that African chiefs went along with the trade. The Europeans always took gifts for them, paid tolls to pass through. In this way the African chiefs supported the trade.

## Socialization and Control

Teachers T (i) and T (ii) in Trinidad and Tobago approached thematic areas of the trade, for example, the Middle Passage, using concepts such as socialization and control.

Teacher T (i) tried to deal with the Middle Passage as part of the total socialization of the enslaved African, from the point of capture up to the plantation.

One teacher looked at the capture of a person and how he or she was made to accept the new life. This was a 'seasoning' or an attempt to break the will of the enslaved, beginning with the humiliation of being placed in confinement. This could result in the loss of self-respect and esteem. He presented the Middle Passage to his students not just as a beginning and end in itself but as part of a greater process of the treatment of the enslaved person. The cruelty of the Middle Passage was part of the socialization of the enslaved.

Teacher T (ii) spoke of the importance of teaching concepts. One concept she used along with socialization was the idea of control. She tried to make her students understand that everything Europeans did had an aspect of control to it – whether in terms of the ship; the plantation; the numbers of enslaved persons; the fact they did not understand the culture of the people they were enslaving. Teacher T(II) identified the concepts of control and justice as being a focal point in her teaching.

## GETTING THE MESSAGE ACROSS
## TEACHING STRATEGIES EMPLOYED: MOST EFFECTIVE STRATEGIES

### Multidisciplinary approach

A multidisciplinary approach to teaching the TTEA was adopted at the school of Teacher A in the UK. At this London school, the departments involved in teaching the subject included the music, textile, arts, humanities and English departments. The cross-curricular links benefited from the resources of the school's humanities department.

Teacher R in the USA explained that the special curriculum for the TTEA, prepared by the African and Multicultural Studies Department of New Orleans Public Schools, was infused into the regular curriculum. The classes used to deliver the special curriculum included social studies and English.

Administrator 2 in the USA felt that a multidisciplinary approach facilitated greater rapport with the students than was normally the case. He was of the view that the only way of introducing the subject of the trade to students, in his context, was to interweave the formal curricula with non-formal learning experiences like field trips to historic Places of Memory, as well as to depict and dramatize the experiences of the enslaved ancestors. This, he said, made for more interesting and factual discussion and would have greater impact on the students.

In Brazil, the trade was taught through geography, history, physics and chemistry. Teacher Q (i) said her students also developed an awareness of African culture through the study of slavery from the work done in the music, textiles, arts and English departments.

### THE ARTS AND CULTURAL MANIFESTATIONS

Administrator 1 in the UK favoured teaching the TTEA through the arts as one area of the positive contributions of the African diaspora. She designed the Youth Forum, held in Bristol in 2001, to examine the trade through the arts. Participants worked on murals, sculpted masks, painting, textiles, song and dance.

In Brazil, the most successful strategy for teaching the trade was showing students its legacies in contemporary Brazilian society. Other teachers also found it effective to highlight the cultural manifestations of the African heritage in Brazil, for example, Carnival, bossa nova, samba and pagoda (a type of Brazilian music). The use of musical instruments, dance such as the *capoeira* (also a form of martial arts), and the erection of flags were also believed to be successful teaching aids. The Brazilian teachers highlight elements which have a strong African influence and are accepted by the other cultures in order to sensitize students to the contributions of Afro-Brazilians.

### CONNECTING, JOURNAL WRITING, POETRY AND ARTISTIC EXPRESSION

Teacher R in the USA as well as Administrator 2 in the USA, were concerned that the TTEA should represent for students 'an intra-relational experience'. Teacher R and her colleagues worked hard to get their students to connect with the experience of the enslaved

Africans. She believed there was nothing separating her students from the experience of the enslaved Africans; that it was just a matter of fate that they were born 400 years later. Had they been in Africa on the west coast 400 years ago, they could have been the ones captured and sold into slavery. She tried to fuse this thinking into the curriculum since her students would never get it in a textbook.

They also tried to get their students to connect current situations with historical ones so they could begin to link the concepts. This proved difficult at the eighth grade level. She focused, therefore, on developing students' skills of comprehending high order thinking and pulling concepts together. She saw the teaching the TTEA as an opportunity to teach students to connect ideas and concepts and in a way that gave life to the textbooks.

While Administrator 2 in the USA encouraged journal writing exercises, this component was the least pursued until the intervention of an academic from a New Orleans university. She started working with the students one-on-one or in small group settings. She worked with them on artistic expression and the students produced what was described as 'a bevy of work' compiled in an excellently done book of poetry which showcased the ways in which the children internalized what they had experienced during the academic year. Teachers R and S agreed that engaging students in writing, with the support and guidance of a university professor and exposing them to primary documents were among the most successful teaching strategies.

The efforts of teachers R and S in the USA to link the history of the trade with their students' current reality were successful. Teacher R explained it was this strategy that resulted in students' active participation in class and in the poetry they wrote because they began to connect those concepts and feel a sense of ownership of the history. Initially, when they discussed slavery, many students did not want to talk about it; it was in the past and they did not want to own their history. She explained that nobody wants to be from Africa, nobody wants to be 'a jungle person'. She saw the need to tear down those stereotypes that are still very evident in students' lives, and which show up in the ugly way in which they speak to one another. Teachers have to use information to try to get rid of the negative ideas that have been indoctrinated in students. When students begin to accept the information imparted to them by their teachers, they become considerably more comfortable with the conversation about slavery and produce wonderful poetry.

Teacher S described the students' poems as being 'really dynamic'. She explained that at first, they were somewhat apprehensive about writing, but that once they started, they did a good job. She shared with the author the following poem written by one student after a class discussion about the abuse that the enslaved Africans had endured:

> ***Am I tired*** by [name of student] – 12 years old
> Am I tired?
> Who should I ask my Master or my Lord?
> My Lord guides me and my Master beats me
> Am I tired?
> Who shall I follow?
> My Lord or my Master?
> My Lord heals me and my Master mistreats me
> Am I tired?
> I made up my mind I can't stay here anymore and let you abuse me.
> I'm going, Now I'm free.

The following poem by another of their students was cause for concern as to whether the student (female) was writing about the abuse of an enslaved woman or about her own abuse. However, the teachers said they both knew the student involved and felt certain she was not being abused, but had written about something with which she empathized. This provides some indication of the value of their attempts to relate the history of the TTEA to their students' reality.

> ***I see Blank*** by [name of student]
> I see blank
> I see blank
> I see blank
> I see blank

*It is Black, I see a woman. She is by the well and a man and he says,*
*"Hold my hand" and says, "Come with me," and she went and they went in a house.*
*An hour later they came out and he says, "Don't tell nobody" and she says, "I will not".*

Teachers in Jamaica also identified creative expression as a successful strategy to support teaching the TTEA.

### ROLE PLAYING, DRAMATIZATION AND REFERRING TO SOURCES

Role playing and dramatization were considered most successful teaching strategies by teachers in Barbados, Jamaica, and Trinidad and Tobago and artistic work and creative expression were highly favoured by teachers in Brazil, Jamaica and the USA. Teachers R and S in the USA used role playing to convey, for example, how enslaved Africans were shipped and for the enactment of the images they found on the Internet. Teacher S explained that students enact being on a slave ship, lying on the floor and entwining their arms.

Teacher T (i) in Trinidad and Tobago identified dramatization as a most successful teaching strategy. In using it, he encouraged students to cite their sources of information and to rely on evidence as opposed to relying on their own feelings, particularly in depicting the cruelty of slavery. He noted that when playing the roles of the enslaved and slave-owner, students tended to enact extreme cruelty on the part of the slave-owner and pain on the part of the enslaved. When evaluating and questioning students he tries to be careful that, to support their portrayals or written work, they rely more on evidence and not on their own feeling.

### EXPOSING STUDENTS TO ACTUAL SOURCES AND HAVING THEM BUILD THEIR OWN INTERPRETATIONS; ALLOWING STUDENTS TO EXPRESS THEIR OWN VIEWS

Teacher N in the USA noted the effectiveness of exposing students to actual sources and having them build their own interpretations. She reported that, for example, she asks her students to read excerpts from different types of sources that will allow them to challenge particular interpretations of aspects of the trade and to develop an African-American point of view on slavery. Once they have used the sources themselves, they are able to discuss why the work of one author is different from that of another. This strategy has proved successful. She concluded that whenever students are able to read sources and develop interpretations of their own, it 'pulls them' into the subject.

In dealing with a thematic area such as the reason that the trade to the Caribbean in enslaved Africans was stopped, Teacher H in the Gambia presented her students with the different perspectives on the theme and then encouraged them to present their own points of view.

## Music

Teacher T (ii) in Trinidad and Tobago stated that, when the opportunity arose, she used calypso to help teach thematic areas such as Haiti. The music of David Rudder, philosopher/calypsonian from Trinidad and Tobago, was mentioned in particular.

## Allowing students' choice

Teacher N in the USA shared her experience that students' individual research based on images could become a basis for further research and provide the class with enough information to discuss issues such as the cooperation of Africans with Europeans in the conduct of the TTEA. The choices made by the students moved the class in certain directions and empowered them. Because they were making different choices, they were learning a great deal from one another. She gave the example of one of her students who chose an image of an African king sitting on a throne surrounded by a multitude of people and in the background there was a European flag. It was depiction of a ceremony. The class was able to find enough information to talk about the fact that it was not only Europeans who were involved in the Trade but that there was some cooperation on the part of the Africans. It was in the process of going through this student's research that the class began talking about the trade. Students' own research interests influenced the content of class discussions. By the time they had all presented their research, they had deepened their knowledge based on the work of their classmates.

## RETURNING TO THE SUBJECT OF THE TRANSATLANTIC TRADE IN ENSLAVED AFRICANS

Teacher N in the USA underscored the critical importance of the study of slavery to the understanding of US history. She returned to the subject of slavery repeatedly to locate it as the foundation of her class. Her strategy of recycling the subject within the history curriculum helped to deal with the problem of inadequate time for teaching it. She approached the subject the first time with the development of the Atlantic world, then again in the colonial era with the idea of racial slavery, returning to it in the antebellum era with the idea of how the institution was changing in the nineteenth century. She felt that having taught the subject through three separate eras, students developed a fairly good understanding of the institution of slavery in the context of the TTEA.

## GROUP WORK, PROJECTS, WORKSHOPS, FIELD TRIPS, OUT OF CLASSROOM AND HANDS-ON EXPERIENCES, GAMES AND QUIZZES

Teachers in the USA, Jamaica, and Trinidad and Tobago found field trips to Places of Memory effective learning experiences. Teacher T (v), Trinidad and Tobago, in particular, emphasized the value of taking students out of the classroom and letting them work on their own, interviewing people and finding information for themselves. From her experience such approaches resulted in students developing a love for history 'because history is a subject most of the children prefer not to have to do, because they say that teachers just give them notes'.

Teachers R and S in the USA also mentioned students' hands-on experience as most successful teaching strategies. Group work and projects were found to be most effective by teachers in Barbados, Benin, Denmark and Senegal. Games, quizzes and workshops were found to be effective by Teachers F and G in Senegal and Benin. Teachers in Brazil also taught their students to investigate and to do field work.

## Consider Alternative Motivations of Personalities in History

Teacher T (i) in Trinidad and Tobago cautioned his students against taking for granted historical interpretations and asked them to consider alternative motivations for the actions of personalities in history. He gave as an example examining the actions of Europeans and Americans in terms of their humanitarian work and trying to find other reasons for them, other than just 'the surface reason'. The fact that there are several books written on the same subject means that people have different perspectives on the issues.

Teacher T (iii) in Trinidad and Tobago supported Teacher T (i) in pointing to the contradictions that might be inherent in the presentation of historical personalities and the fact that these contradictions were not usually pointed out.

## Setting Aside a Special Day to Teach the Transatlantic Trade in Enslaved Africans

As in the case of teachers in the UK in particular, teachers R and S in the USA were expected to teach the state curriculum of which the TTEA was not a part. They therefore set aside a particular day to address the subject.

## Timeline Exercise and Timeframe That Does Not End

To make the theme of the duration of the TTEA more real for students, Teacher C in the UK developed a timeline exercise showing the starting point and the end point.

Taking into account the ongoing cultural legacies of the trade in terms of the music and other art forms of Trinidad and Tobago, Teacher T (iii) in Trinidad and Tobago, on the other hand, tended to 'teach slavery in a timeframe that doesn't end'. As an example of this he recalled teaching a unit on calypso and the 'double entendre' — the means by which people protested in a kind of coded language so they could communicate among themselves and ridicule the slave-owner or governor without their knowledge. When he moved to Trinidad and Tobago in 1982, one of the things he noticed about the people was their ability to talk about another person within earshot of the person without his or her knowledge. This he described as a manifestation of the 'double entendre' of the culture, and is reflected in the calypso art form of Trinidad and Tobago. To put a timeframe on the TTEA, therefore, would be to circumscribe it within the physical actuality of the trade itself. But then the cultural and social aspects of the legacies of the trade are worth exploring if only to make sense of the kind of cultural fusion that exists. The steel pan and calypso are legacies that tend to make teaching the TTEA relevant today.

## COLLABORATION WITH EUROPEAN COLLEAGUES AND ELECTRONIC LINKAGES

For teaching the concept of the TTEA as a European turning point, Teacher B in the UK explained that in order to meet the requirements of the national curriculum they had to consider what the other European countries were doing and they were consequently 'very reliant on colleagues in Denmark, Norway and in Holland'. One of the benefits of such international linkages would be to have lessons on the subject developed in the countries that were involved in the trade. At the same time, the UK teachers were sending information to these European colleagues about Bristol. Electronic linkages were also considered as potential support for teaching the subject as the websites of the schools in these countries tended to be very good.

## USE OF MAPS

Teacher C in the UK used maps to illustrate the Triangular Trade and its three cargo types. Teachers in Brazil, and Trinidad and Tobago also spoke of using maps to support their teaching. Teacher T (ii) in Trinidad and Tobago noted the effectiveness of visuals such as maps in teaching the TTEA and in developing students' skills in gathering evidence. She noted that students tended to appreciate the use of maps and statistics that showed different tribes and where they came from.

## Telling the Story from the Perspective of the Enslaved Africans

Teacher N in the USA emphasized how long it has taken to begin to tell the story from the perspective of the enslaved and not only from that of the slave-owners. She encouraged her students to learn using all sorts of sources and creative methods.

## Teaching Resources

### Images, film, videos

Teacher B in the UK used images 'such as those in a Norwegian book about the slave ship, the Fredensborg' and cartoons from the period to support teaching themes such as 'How Slaves Were Shipped'. He identified the very strong Clarkson image, classic in British textbooks, portraying enslaved Africans packed into the hull of the slave ship as an effective image to show students how the enslaved Africans were shipped. This image hangs on the wall of the British Industrial Museum and has been found to have a powerful impact as it communicates a sense of lack of space, lack of privacy, lack of human dignity.

Teacher H in the Gambia also used this image of a slave ship, *The Brooks*, first produced for the abolitionist campaign in eighteenth century England and reproduced by UNESCO in the form of a poster distributed to all schools participating in its Associated Schools Transatlantic Slave Trade Education Project.

Teacher C in the UK used 'sources such as Clarkson and Newton' to support teaching the theme 'The number of enslaved Africans a typical slave ship crossing the Atlantic carried,' plus images and video.

The movie *Amistad* was used by several teachers to support classroom teaching. In addition to video and picture sources, Teacher A in the UK used this film to support teaching themes such as 'How slave ships were powered' (though this was not one of the original themes used in this study) and 'How enslaved Africans were shipped.' Teacher E in Denmark also used this film as he found it helped students to visualize the trade. It was used as a point of departure. In Trinidad and Tobago, Teacher T (iii) also used *Amistad* and prepared a form that students could complete while viewing it, to better appreciate the role of the characters in relation to the trade. Using this approach students were able to reflect on the nature of the various characters' involvement in the trade. They reflected on the perspectives of the enslaved or the abolitionist, for example, and he categorizes the various personalities according to the concepts that he wants to teach.

Teacher C in the UK identified the use of videos as the most effective strategy in teaching the trade because this medium communicates the horror of the Middle Passage and the inhumanity of the auction sale. The students are able to see clearly the unfair actions and beliefs of the white slave traders. Both Teachers A and C in the UK observed that students did not respond to statistics in isolation but that they related much better to images.

## Drawings and paintings

Teacher N in the USA used drawings and paintings to illustrate the different sources which could be used in the study of slavery. The drawings and paintings were used to discuss why they would have been created and what could and could not be learned from them. They were also used to stimulate students' research. Some students were more interested in the enslavement process, some in the Middle Passage and some intrigued by what happened when they first got to the New World. Through students' research the class generated information on many of the initial questions about the supply of slaves, the presence of Africans in Western Europe and how enslaved Africans were shipped. A painting, which a student found of an enslaved person being beaten in the street with a church with the cross in the background stimulated a discussion about how it was possible that Christians could enslave people. Teacher N explained that this was not a strong student but the image juxtaposing Christianity with slavery moved her to start researching.

## Guest speakers

Guest speakers were invited to address the students at the New Orleans public school. Each quarter there was a 'nomo series' emphasizing the regenerative power of the spoken word. Administrator 2 in the USA believed that this came out of the Twi language and was also found in many other West African lexicons. Ninety per cent of the speakers were from a New Orleans university. The university provided topic consultants, professors of history primarily, who talked about specific issues related to the content areas they were pursuing. One guest speaker from the history department of the university spoke to the students about life on the average Southern plantation. Experts in the areas of movement, theatre and story telling were also brought in.

In teaching about the Maroons, teachers in Jamaica invited a representative of the Maroon community to address their students and share information about the Maroon heritage and culture in Jamaica. At the national level, Jamaica observes Heritage Week and this helps expose students to Maroon culture and history through visits to related heritage sites.

## Places of Memory

In Brazil, Jamaica and the USA students were also taken on visits to relevant Places of Memory. Teacher J (ii) in Jamaica indicated that on visits to heritage sites reflective of the Maroon history, the Maroon colonel would talk about the Maroons and take them to places where the Maroons actually lived and operated. The Department of African and Multicultural Studies within the New Orleans public school system also operated a programme known as 'Kids to Africa'. Under this programme, students visited slave castles at Elmina and Cape Coast in Ghana. Videos and slides of those visits were shown to other students. A member of the Department also spoke to the students about the dungeons at the Elmina and Cape Coast castles.

Teacher G in Benin also highlighted the impact of visits to Places of Memory. Students were very interested in these outings. At each Place of Memory they learned about 'the drama that unfolded in the slave trade'. After the outing, each student had to submit a written report and this report is graded.

## The Internet and Online Resources

Teacher N in the USA used the Internet and on-line resources to provide students with a choice as to what they could select for further exploration. Through these resources her class enjoys access to the narratives of Frederick Douglass and approximately two hundred other narratives of the enslaved from which they can choose. She described the availability of choice as an advantage of being in a small classroom and having access to the technology, particularly when there was not enough time to explore some of the topics in-depth.

In discussing statistical data such as the numbers of enslaved Africans carried on a slave ship, Teacher N in the USA would begin with the image of a slave ship, using a recently acquired database compiled by David Eltis and others. She noted that once her students had seen the image of the slave ship, the typical question that followed related to the number of enslaved Africans it carried. From her experience she found that starting with images and music 'drew the kids in', as opposed to starting with a textbook. Like Teacher A in the UK, she observed that her students did not respond to cold statistical information.

## Original Documents, Primary Sources, Slave Narratives and Texts

Teacher A in the UK, Teachers R and S in the USA, and Teacher T (ii) in Trinidad and Tobago used primary sources of information including original documents and slave narratives.

Teacher N in the USA used narratives such as the antebellum narrative *Meredith* and the narrative of Frederick Douglass. She also planned to use a section of Frederick Douglass' longer autobiography *My Bondage, My Freedom* in which he discussed the ways in which slavery affected his relationship with his mother, his grandmother and his aunts. Additionally, she made use of an online database of about 200 slave narratives produced by a professor of English at the University of North Carolina and who had written the introduction to Frederick Douglass' *My Bondage, My Freedom*. Teacher R in the USA also used the Frederick Douglass narrative to support her efforts at relating the history of the TTEA to students' realities.

Elaborating on her use of primary documents Teacher T (ii) in Trinidad and Tobago explained that students needed to learn the skills of a student historian; what historians do in compiling the evidence they need, the secondary resources available in the form of books, for example. The students appreciated that. They tended to respond more and she urged them when writing anything, to make references to the primary sources and not only to the secondary texts.

## TEXTBOOKS

Teacher B in the UK described British textbooks as 'good' and 'terrific' for teaching the Middle Passage, but noted that they had little about the Maroons. Teachers R and N in the USA, however, found that the available textbooks were ineffective and tended to treat superficially some thematic areas of the historiography of the TTEA.

Teacher N in the USA, though admitting that she did not like textbooks, nevertheless mentioned a few texts which she consulted in her teaching. These included *Slavery* by Stanley Oaken, which discussed plantation records and argued that 'slavery was so dehumanizing; that the slave system was so repressive, that it rendered slaves as childlike.' She countered this text with one by John Blassingame who wrote about slave culture and looked at the slave narrative. This teacher was critical of texts which treated the subject of the TTEA superficially. She expressed the view that their way of incorporating slavery into a narrative of US history was to 'stick in the words to a slave song on one page', which was more degrading than leaving it out entirely.

Teacher R in the USA remarked that some of the texts used left students unaware of what brought enslaved Africans to the USA. She observed that such textbooks gloss over what actually happened 'and the children have this concept that slaves just arrived here'.

Despite her dislike for textbooks Teacher N in the USA nonetheless used them to illustrate, for example, the different ways in which they treated topics such as the Middle Passage. In addition to Stanley Oaken and John Blassingame, she mentioned Phillip Curtin as being useful in supporting her teaching. She also used online sources to complement the use of textbooks.

Among the secondary texts used by Teacher T (ii) in Trinidad and Tobago was Shirley Gordon's (1983) *Caribbean Generations* to develop the skills of the student historian, and to encourage students to use a number of sources to formulate their own opinions. She explained that Gordon's text presented students with extracts conveying, for example, the point of view of the enslaved and the point of view of a captain of a slave ship. Students have to determine the author of the extracts in question, the reasons that particular points of view are being expressed and make their own judgements on the issues at hand.

Other specific texts and authors some teachers mentioned as enriching teaching included: *Black Jacobins* by C.L.R James; *Capitalism and Slavery* by Eric Williams, (Teacher T (i) Trinidad and Tobago); and *The Diary of Thomas Thistlewood* (Teacher T (ii) in Trinidad and Tobago). Text and technology resources used by the teachers interviewed, are summarized below.

SUMMARY OF SOME TEXT AND TECHNOLOGY RESOURCES USED BY TEACHERS

- Videos, e.g. the *Roots* series (UK)
- Slave Narratives — *Meredith*, the narrative of Frederick Douglass and his larger autobiography *My Bondage, My Freedom* (USA)
- Pictures and Posters (UK, USA)
- Textbooks mentioned: *Slavery*, by Stanley Oaken, (USA); *Caribbean Generations* by Shirley Gordon (Trinidad and Tobago); *Slave Voices* by Hilary Beckles and Verene Shepherd (eds.) (Benin and Senegal); *Slave Voyages: The Trade in Enslaved Africans* by Hilary Beckles (The Gambia, Trinidad and Tobago)
- Authors mentioned: Phillip Curtin (USA), John Blassingame (USA), C.L.R. James (Trinidad and Tobago), Eric Williams (Trinidad and Tobago)
- Maps (Brazil, Jamaica, UK)

- Statistics (Denmark, Trinidad and Tobago, USA)
- CD-Roms, Internet Sources and Powerpoint (USA)

## Factors Impacting on Teachers' Delivery of Content Knowledge

### Establishing the Relevance of the Transatlantic Trade in Enslaved Africans

In Denmark there was no obligation to teach the TTEA. Teacher E taught the subject because he thought 'it was very interesting and relevant' and facilitated an understanding of the development of parts of the world. The Danish education system permitted teachers to teach a subject if they considered it to be essential and interesting for the students. Teachers themselves decided on major areas of focus for a particular academic year.

### Teachers' knowledge, interest and passion

Administrator 2 in the USA alluded to the possibility that teachers involved in the Project might not have been well informed on the subject of the Transatlantic Trade in Enslaved Africans but that its impact was such that the teachers grew in knowledge, just as their students did.

Teachers R and S in the USA, neither of whom was a history teacher, explained that they were able to implement the UNESCO Associated Schools Transatlantic Slave Trade Education Project because they were avid readers and 'participate at some level with African American history'. They also exposed themselves to training opportunities in order to benefit their students. This was an extension of who they are. Many of them participated in a workshop on *Amistad* research projects designed for teachers. They take advantage of professional development opportunities in order to provide for their students learning opportunities that cannot be had by using textbooks, about which they expressed some measure of distrust.

Teacher N in the USA had done a summer programme which looked at slavery from a comparative perspective and it really opened her eyes to the fact that she was teaching slavery from a US perspective. She believed it would take her some time to integrate enough of the subject into her class but felt that the summer programme was the kind of class that changes a teacher's perspective on how to teach. She was quite passionate about teaching her US history class and was eager to work with her colleagues to adopt a broader perspective to the subject.

Referring to the questionnaire used by UNESCO to assess students' knowledge of the subject of the TTEA, Teacher E in Denmark made the point that the information his students did not know, he did not know either.

There was some content knowledge that Teacher H in the Gambia did not know nor had she ever come across in the process of her own education. Referring to the text *Slave Voyages* by Hilary Beckles, prepared for schools in the UNESCO Associated Schools Transatlantic Slave Trade Education Project, she stated that the history books to which she had been exposed did not focus much on the Caribbean.

## IMPORTANCE OF TEACHERS' KNOWLEDGE

Teachers' confidence in imparting content knowledge was likely to be heightened once their own knowledge base was assured, as evident in a statement by T (i) of Trinidad and Tobago, who 'had the benefit of doing West African history with Dr. Fitz Baptiste' at The University of the West Indies. He felt that he could rely on this background in West African history and link it with Caribbean history in his teaching.

## TEACHERS NEED HELP

Teacher I (iii) in Barbados wanted writers 'to help students and teachers to some extent' in the ways in which information about the origins of enslaved Africans, for example, was presented. Given the reality of new African countries, teachers experienced difficulty in mapping certain ethnic groups without the benefit of having done courses that would have taught them what the African map or groupings were in the seventeenth century and their modern equivalent. As an example of this she referred to speaking to students about the Gold Coast and when they go to the map they see Ghana.

## TEACHER TRAINING

Teacher D, a teacher trainer at a Bristol university in the UK, trained teachers to teach the TTEA within the confines of the national history curriculum. The context was the history course of the Post-Graduate Certificate of Education (PGCE). This course lasted 12 weeks and the trainee teachers had 11 hours of tutoring per week. Of this time, amounting to a total of 132 hours, one five hour session was spent on preparing the trainee teachers to teach black history. By the end of the day, it was hoped that they would be able to produce two lessons on an aspect of black history. These trainee teachers were described by Teacher D as being unique in having this experience as this was not usually done. Usually, trainee teachers received no training in teaching black history in the UK context. He hoped that they would be able to share what they learned with other teachers and tried to ensure that they had some material to support them in their teaching. But for this brief exposure they generally knew little or nothing about the TTEA.

Trainee teachers in this programme were provided with a range of strategies to use. They could access black history websites. The teacher trainer also sent them newsletters which included references to particularly good websites.

The areas of focus in the five hours of the teacher training history course spent on black history were slavery, resistance and Africa before the TTEA, the last area being given greatest emphasis. Ultimately, however, there was no guarantee that once the trainee teachers secured jobs as teachers, they would actually teach these elements of black history. The approach used was not to actually cover subject content. Rather, the focus was on 'how people teach' and the opportunities for teaching black history as there was no requirement for it to be taught.

There was a tendency for teachers in all three regions – the Americas and the Caribbean, Africa and Europe – to focus on strategies they employed to teach even as they discussed what content they taught. This established a very interesting parallel with the statement of Teacher D in the UK, whose university course did not actually cover subject content, but concentrated instead on 'how people teach' and these teachers' inclination to also focus on how they taught even as they reflected on what they taught. Indeed, this is at the core of Shulman's (1987) concept of pedagogical content knowledge, and serves to highlight the process of reasoning engaged in by these teachers in teaching the subject.

Teacher D in the UK was of the view that there was a need to build teachers' confidence to teach black history and to provide appropriate materials for use in the classroom. He felt that 'teachers won't teach something until they feel they have the confidence' as well as books which can be used in the classroom. He indicated that most teachers in Britain would not have had the training which would give them the confidence to teach black history, and teachers need that sort of confidence. They need confidence and drive to be able to determine how to integrate the TTEA in their teaching. Consequently, one of the functions of integrating the subject in the PGCE course was to offer teachers some materials; and with materials which they can use in classes, comes confidence.

## TEACHER DEVELOPMENT AND TEACHERS SHARING THEIR EXPERIENCES

Teacher I (iii) in Barbados spoke of the impact her participation in the UNESCO International Youth Forum on the TTEA in Senegal had on her teaching, and specifically in relation to the role of Gorée Island in the trade. Since visiting Gorée Island, she treated this thematic area with greater meaning and in greater detail. The opportunity to participate in the UNESCO Project, the visit to Senegal and the materials provided by UNESCO to support teaching the subject all contributed to her ongoing professional development as a teacher.

Referring to the author's interview with the focus group, she described the exchanges with her colleague teachers as being beneficial. In her comments there was recognition and appreciation of the possibilities which existed for teachers to learn from the experiences of one another.

## Challenges Encountered in Teaching the Transatlantic Trade in Enslaved Africans

Teachers pointed to several challenges impacting on their successful teaching of the TTEA.

### Successful Implementation of an Interdisciplinary Approach

Teacher F in Senegal felt that the greatest challenge to teaching the subject was the successful implementation of an interdisciplinary approach that would allow teachers to deal with the different aspects of the trade in their class through literature, science, mathematics, history and geography, for example. This is a challenge because not everyone understands the importance of teaching the subject or knows how to treat with it.

### Lack of Suitable Textbooks and Need for More Images

On the issue of textbooks and images, teachers identified several challenges: the inadequacy of available textbooks (Teacher B, UK; Teacher I(i), Barbados); finding sources appropriate for 'lower ability students' (Teacher C, UK); suitable material in sufficient quantities (Teacher J (i), Jamaica); attractively presented texts with language suitable for the average student, and not requiring too much preparation on the part of teachers; finding workbooks already developed for teachers (Teacher I (i), Barbados); and greater access to images to enhance students' understanding of the subject (Administrator 1, UK, Teacher H, the Gambia).

Teacher B in the UK, commenting on the inadequacy of some available textbooks, noted that they do not cover more than two pages on slavery - Nothing on African culture, nothing on the legacies of slavery and very little on abolition. 'A second page spread, because of lack of resources, that's what we're limited to,' he said, adding that quite often teachers would not use such materials because of their limited, negative depiction.

Teacher D in the UK, a teacher trainer, underscoring the lack of resources and suitable books as factors contributing to the absence of the subject in schools in the UK explained the need to recognize that teachers themselves had not studied the subject at university and that they did not have books other than 'huge books that take a week to get to'. Teachers cannot afford the time needed to go through long books so there is a real need for books that cater to teachers' specific needs and that can be used in the classroom.

Teacher B in the UK added that while the UNESCO Associated Schools 'Transatlantic Slave Trade Education Project' facilitated access to schools and to more resources, there remained the difficulty of 'finding things at the right level for children', given their reading level. A great deal of money had been invested to adapt materials to the appropriate level, but, he said, 'it takes time' and was not easy. Similar challenges were articulated by Teachers I (i) and I (ii) in Barbados. Teacher I (i) pointed out that sometimes there is not enough material written for children; that it is not every student who will be doing CXC and asked, 'Why are all the books written for CXC?' She advocated producing attractive books on the subject of the trade for students with colourful pictures, and using language that would not be too challenging for average students who make up the majority of students. This would pre-empt the need for teachers to have to modify and simplify texts, which cuts into their teaching time.

She added that an average student cannot handle fine print; that a teacher did not necessarily want to keep teaching the subject in the same way and that the availability of workbooks on the subject, for example, would therefore provide a good alternative. There was also a need for more technological resources catering to students to support teaching the subject.

Teacher H, in the Gambia commented on the availability of many written accounts and the need for more images which would be able to communicate more effectively to students. Teachers in the UK also wanted more images. Additionally they wanted to see the role of women heightened, and more case studies of individuals, such as Olaudah Equiano.

INADEQUATE TIME FOR RESEARCH AND FOR TEACHING

Inadequate time for teachers to do research was presented as a challenge for teachers in Barbados. Inadequate teaching time was a challenge for teachers in Trinidad and Tobago, the UK and the USA.

For Teacher N in the USA the challenge was in finding enough time for students to develop an emotional attachment to the subject. Teacher A in the UK drew attention to the 'small amount of teaching time' that was actually spent on teaching the subject at her school. Within a unit of work of about 40 lessons in a little less than a term, the curriculum only allowed for seven hours teaching the subject. Teacher B, in the UK reiterated this point in relation to teaching slavery in Brazil, for example. He commented, 'We're zooming through...quite fast...so we don't have time to cover all of those theories.' Teacher N in the USA explained that, as important as she considers the TTEA, she has an obligation to get to Vietnam and the space age and even then she has to be selective. The challenge was also to give her students an opportunity to discover some of the information on their own, so that their learning was not reduced to merely picking up a textbook and reading through the chapters and 'spitting it back on a test'. She wanted them to have a deeper understanding of the subject within a certain amount of time and students, even 15, 16, and 17 year-olds, need some time. When a teacher flies through a subject, students do not have time to develop an emotional attachment to or a full understanding of the subject; rather, they are simply memorizing.

Teacher T (i), Trinidad and Tobago, had to try very hard to be as comprehensive as possible in the limited teaching time available, and to get his students to understand certain concepts. He was of the view that with time constraints, instead of finding different ways of teaching the subject and making it interesting and really getting the students involved, the majority of teachers tended to just present students with the information and move on; they did not attempt to ascertain the nature of students' responses to the information or whether they could use additional teaching resources such as might be available via the Internet. Indeed, teachers might not have access to the Internet in their classrooms nor have easy access to the school's computer room and the majority of children might not have Internet access at home. Although teachers want to broaden their students' understanding of the subject they might not have the time to do so.

## TEACHERS' POOR SELF-IMAGE

Teacher T (i), Trinidad and Tobago, expressed concern about teachers' own contradictions which arise out of their socialization. While teachers may teach 'from an academic perspective,' he said, 'deep down we have this image of ourselves as was fostered by the experience of slavery.' Because of socialization and even after the Black Power experience of the 1970s which sought to improve the status of the person of African heritage in the society, Afro-Trinidadian students still used the term 'black' with a negative connotation.

Teacher T (i) observed that while the preferential treatment of persons of lighter complexion seemed to have disappeared, he found that such value systems had re-emerged. He was of the view that this came right back to the question of the legacies of slavery and that, unless there was a really concerted and continuous effort to teach the TTEA and its legacies, many people would continue to experience pain and suffering.

## STUDENTS APPRECIATING DIFFERENT PERSPECTIVES ON HISTORY

Having his students appreciate that there was never only one interpretation or perspective on any period of history, was for Teacher E in Denmark one of his greatest challenges. For him 'things are never black and white', there is never one side only. In teaching the TTEA, it seemed there were only good guys and bad guys which he did not feel to be the case. He felt it was always important to understand the reasons certain events took place and that history was over-simplified if discussed in a polarity that fails to be relevant today. In teaching the subject, therefore, he always asks his students to relate the content presented to contemporary society and to assess its usefulness in today's world.

## APPRECIATING THE VALUE OF KNOWING ONE'S ANCESTRY; OWNING THE HISTORY OF THE TRANSATLANTIC TRADE IN ENSLAVED AFRICANS

Teachers R and S in the USA described their greatest challenge as getting their students 'to buy into the concept of understanding the enslaved people'. The beginning of the process, they explained, was the most difficult part: getting the students to understand the concept of slavery, getting them to want to understand and to appreciate the value of knowing about their ancestry. This was painful for their students and sometimes they did not feel that they could handle it. According to Teacher S, 'Once they do buy into it, it's wonderful, but getting them to do it initially is hard.'

This was also a challenge for Teacher N in the USA, at her all female, predominantly white, elite New Orleans school. Her challenge was getting her students to recognize that the history of the TTEA was a part of their own history; that it was not black history but American history.

## Getting students involved in projects

The teachers in Barbados described the challenges in getting students, and especially their male students, involved in projects. Students were given the opportunity to design things if they were good at art, use computers and the Internet, sing songs, make up jingles, but students were generally not responsive. Some of them became involved only when they were preparing for a tour to Bristol, UK. They were asked to present some art material, a collage. For this project they collected the information and they spent a great deal of time in the art room.

## Students expressing their own views and thinking critically

Among the teachers in Jamaica, a difficulty was getting students to express their own views, to think critically and to be analytical. Students were described as being able to answer questions based on recall – factual information they can read in a book — but when asked to express their own opinion using evidence from the literature, it was hard to get them to be critically analytic.

## Lack of adequate Places of Memory

Teacher T (ii) in Trinidad and Tobago found it difficult to engage with the history of the TTEA through physical evidence of the legacies of slavery in Trinidad and Tobago, as would be found in Places of

Memory. A larger number of preserved Places of Memory existed in other Caribbean islands such as the Dominican Republic and St. Croix, and she underscored the value of these in supporting teaching the subject to enable students to identify with the fact that Trinidad experienced slavery and was involved in sugar production. She felt that her students were at a disadvantage not being able to see the artefacts associated with slavery, to have that lived experience.

## OTHER CHALLENGES

Teacher N in the USA identified several other challenges. These were: providing students with an opportunity to learn on their own; coordinating with colleagues who teach history to locate US History in a global context; and upgrading her own knowledge of the subject area.

For the Brazilian teachers the challenge was to determine the limits of diversity and to have their students accept the concept of being 'different but equal'. In Jamaica, financial costs involved in taking students on field trips presented a challenge.

Difficulties accessing the Internet, and teaching West African civilization were other challenges identified in Trinidad and Tobago. With regard to the latter, Teacher T (ii) was not sure that what she taught in any way helped to change her students' perceptions of Africa which they got from television, so that they would appreciate that there was a West African civilization. She believed that, although many of them appreciate the fact that Africa had a civilization, the images projected on television of poverty and underdevelopment in Africa were more powerful than what she taught in the classroom.

## SUMMARY

The main themes around which content knowledge of the Transatlantic Trade in Enslaved Africans was organized included: slavery as a long established idea and the TTEA as a European turning point; the positive contributions of Africans; slave transportation in the triangular slave trade; 'the African situation' and involvement of Africans in the trade. Concepts included: the enslaved African; the humanity of the enslaved African; overcoming hardship; the myth of the passivity of enslaved Africans; valuing the African race; Afrocentrism; and socialization and control.

Teachers employed a diversity of teaching strategies. Multidisciplinary approaches were emphasized as well as the arts. Imagery (pictures, drawings, paintings), both prints and material accessed from the Internet, were used as well as videos and film. Minimum use was made of a timeline exercise. Several teachers spoke to the value of the use of maps. Group work and project work proved popular in most cases.

Field trips to Places of Memory were undertaken in those countries where such places were easier to identify than in Trinidad and Tobago, for example, where much of this kind of living history was said to be lost. Developing students' 'high order thinking' and their ability to identify and appreciate concepts as a means of learning were concerns expressed by a few teachers.

Students were encouraged to cite their sources of information as evidence of their views and opinions (Teacher T(i), Trinidad and Tobago). Role-playing and dramatization were used to a fair degree. However, only one teacher, (Teacher N, in the USA,) allowed students choice in their learning. She also proved unique in her recycling of the subject through the history curriculum, both to centre slavery in US history and to overcome the problem of limited teaching time.

Teachers identified a range of strategies which they considered to be most successful in teaching the TTEA. These included group work or group projects; field trips to Places of Memory; role playing and dramatization; artistic work; creative expression and exposing students to actual sources and having them build their own interpretation.

The challenges of teaching the TTEA, as identified by teachers, included the following:

- access to appropriate teaching and learning resources, principally text and technology resources and images;
- appreciating the complexities of the trade, that things are never 'black and white';
- appreciating African heritage and identity;
- reinterpreting the history of the trade from the perspective of

the enslaved Africans;
- presenting US history from a more global perspective;
- upgrading teachers' knowledge of the subject;
- having sufficient time to teach, so that students would develop an emotional attachment to the subject, and time for teachers to do research in preparation for teaching;
- teaching from a multidisciplinary perspective;
- students researching information on their own, as a means of learning;
- students expressing their own views and thinking critically and analytically;
- access to computers and the Internet;
- changing students' perceptions about West Africa to have them appreciate that there had been a West African civilization;
- access to Places of Memory (in Trinidad and Tobago) to support teaching the subject.

Even within the constraints of their official curriculum, several of these teachers can be considered like the Maroons in their efforts to escape the restrictions of their education system, where teaching the TTEA is concerned. This characteristic of educational *marronage* seemed to be inspired by their concern to ensure the relevance of their teaching to their students' human development needs such as appreciating their ancestry and valuing their identity as descendants of Africans, where applicable; developing survival skills to deal with poverty and adversity; and a general appreciation of the modern world, shaped by living socioeconomic and cultural legacies of a significant phenomenon in history.

The insight of Teacher D, in the UK, a teacher trainer, that teachers will not teach something until they have the confidence and appropriate resources for classroom use, and which was confirmed by several teachers in different countries, sends a strong signal for the need for specially designed teacher training interventions for teaching the subject.

Chapter 5 has examined the organization of content knowledge on the history of the TTEA in the classroom setting. Such organization required a degree of radicalism on the part of some teachers and notably teachers in the UK. Themes and concepts served as organizing principles and myriad teaching strategies served as means of organization. These were quite varied and particularly so in the USA. Ongoing professional development of teachers was recognized as an important element in teachers' ability to organize and impart content knowledge with depth and full understanding. The chapter has also explored strategies found to be most effective in teaching the subject, emergent resource issues, and the greatest challenges for teachers, all of which impacted upon teachers' organization of content knowledge on the TTEA. Though not singled out as a challenge, students' emotional response to content knowledge of the trade nonetheless, proved to be an area of concern.

Chapter 6

# Emotional Dimensions

The manifestations of memory are likely to contribute to evoking an emotional response in teaching and learning about the TTEA. This chapter addresses some of the emotional dimensions of the pedagogical content knowledge of the selected teachers.

It discusses teachers' assessment of students' emotions in the process of their learning about the TTEA, as well as four students' descriptions of their own emotional responses. Inevitably, there is some discussion of teachers' own emotions. The chapter culminates with some insights into some of the emotional dimensions of teachers' pedagogical content knowledge of the TTEA.

## Introduction

These findings are presented according to the category of emotion, and teachers and students' geographic origin. In the cases of Trinidad and Tobago and the UK, a questionnaire was used to solicit additional comments on teachers' observations about the emotional dimension of teaching the subject. These responses are incorporated with teachers' comments obtained from the interviews conducted. They are drawn from the same group of teachers who were interviewed for the study which informs the content of this publication. Since the teachers responding to this questionnaire did so anonymously, they will not be referred to by a code but rather, in general terms, when drawing upon this data. Otherwise, for data obtained on the basis of interviews, teachers will be referred to by the codes used in the rest of the text. This chapter also draws on the views of a few students in Barbados taken from samples of their written work and includes data from four students, two males and two females based on interviews conducted in Denmark and Jamaica.

## An Emotive and Difficult Topic to Teach

Teachers in the Caribbean acknowledged the emotive nature of the topic of the TTEA. One teacher in Barbados expressed the view that it was not possible to teach the subject without having to deal with the full range of emotions such as anger, horror, fear, sadness and disbelief.

A UK teacher expressed a similar opinion and stated that the topic was sure to affect those teaching and being taught. However, the same teacher appeared somewhat uncertain about what the nature of the emotional response might be and noted that it should not be more problematic than teaching about the holocaust and its decimation of the Jews.

Teacher A in the UK explained that she found the topic 'very difficult to present', particularly given the age of her students, just 12 years old. Teaching them about the TTEA was difficult because she was really teaching them about their families and they found it hard to have to admit that for hundreds of years this trade was being conducted. For this teacher it was hard to teach about human tragedy. However, an effort was made to approach the subject with sensitivity. She explained that she and her colleagues endeavoured to engage students in discussion and to allow them space to think about what they were learning. Nonetheless, the topic did prove to be emotive for students. When students viewed the film *Amistad* for example, she said they 'watched and cried…The images of the movie speak to them.' The students were learning a very negative history about themselves and they did not really want to learn about it. They expressed ambivalence. She implied that the context of learning about this history, one in which black students were being taught by white teachers, added to the difficulty of the experience for the students.

Teacher E in Denmark, commenting on his students' emotional responses to the subject, noted that animated emotional discussions in the classroom could be very difficult to handle in terms of the hostile, sometimes dangerous, manner in which students might respond to one another. He noted that it could easily stir up disharmony among them but that this was not unusual with sensitive subjects.

Teachers from Benin and Senegal elaborated that it was not possible to teach the subject without dealing with the atrocities committed against the enslaved Africans: their life in slave dungeons; the terrible treatment meted out to them; the shackles; the horrific journey; their life. When they died, they were thrown overboard to the sharks. When they rebelled, they were killed, mutilated, limbs were amputated, things of this nature. All these are the aspects they insisted upon presenting because they show the reality of the enslaved and this arouses resentment and deep-seated anger in students, even to the point of turning against the teacher.

## SOME GENERAL POINTS

### *TEACHERS' OBJECTIVITY AND BALANCE*

Teachers, especially female teachers, seem to feel a responsibility not to succumb to the emotive aspect of the TTEA, but to be balanced in their treatment of the subject matter with their students. This was particularly the case with teachers interviewed from Barbados, Jamaica and the Gambia who are all female. They felt they needed to suppress their own emotions. They had to be careful not to show prejudice or bias and to draw to students' attention the fact that Africans participated in the enslavement of their own people and that whites were also very instrumental in helping to abolish 'this evil trade.' Theirs was an overwhelming concern to try to remain unbiased in dealing with these facts, although historians tell us that sometimes Africans were left no alternative but to participate in the trade or face armed attacks from neighbouring rival tribes.

J (i), in Jamaica made the point that after teaching the subject for some time teachers may reach a stage where they are able to deal with it and look at it objectively. I (i) in Barbados was acutely aware of the concern of Barbadian society about the subject being taught in an unbalanced manner, and the potential negative impact this could have on students. She commented that had teachers in Barbados not been balanced in their presentation of the subject, students would have been 'showing aggression' Rather, they seemed to accept it as information about which they are unaware. J (ii) in Jamaica stressed students' sensitivity on the subject and their tendency to describe whites as wicked people when they learn about the trade. She reiterated that this pointed to the need to be balanced.

Students in the Gambia tend to respond with disgust, also describing Europeans as 'wicked'. Like the teachers in the English-speaking Caribbean, H from the Gambia indicated that she tried to bring balance to her students' perspectives when they attempt to cast all the blame for the TTEA on the Europeans. She engaged her students in thinking about the role of the Africans themselves in the trade, promoting the perspective that if the Africans did not sell enslaved Africans, the Europeans would not have bought them.

For one male teacher from the UK, objectivity and balance seemed to be expressed in terms of adopting a clinical approach to injustice. He said he did not believe that he had an emotional perspective and that injustice and evil need to be addressed in a clear way and not hidden. He felt it necessary to understand the circumstances in which ordinary people ignored, participated in or were kept unaware of injustice, so that young people might avoid this in the future.

## Impact of Teaching Methodology

T (iv) in Trinidad and Tobago believed that students' emotional reactions depended on the teaching methodology employed. She had observed that students became more emotionally engaged with the history of the TTEA if they were taken out of the classroom to visit places of memory where they are able to see, for example, some of the work done on the sugar factories and where the Africans lived in comparison to where the whites lived. As opposed to listening to the teacher in the classroom, they reacted differently to such learning opportunities and experienced a greater sense of personal connection with the history. She noted that students' emotional response was usually one of anger and they tended to want to know a bit more about the history of their ancestors.

## Teachers' Avoidance of Feelings and Avoidance of Teaching the Transatlantic Trade in Enslaved Africans

T (ii) in Trinidad and Tobago indicated that she does not solicit her students' emotions on the subject. She explained that she tried not to question them too much about their feelings.

T (iii) in Trinidad and Tobago said he had heard reports when discussing the unit on the TTEA in the CXC syllabus, that teachers do not teach the subject for fear of inciting reactions which they may not be able to manage; reactions that might cause animosity among children from different backgrounds. Some teachers were a little wary of introducing a subject 'that might engender a hate, or a reaction, or stereotyping, or prejudice so they prefer to keep to the other units' ..., he said.

## Teachers' Pain, Conflicting Emotions, Religious Views, Concern for Social Justice

T (i) in Trinidad and Tobago shared his feelings of pain, hurt and conflicting emotions caused by the history of the TTEA and his questioning of Christianity as a faith for people of African descent. The emotional dimension of the subject affected his 'other intellectual...experiences' something which he believes also occurs with his students. He observed as well the tendency in the society for people to want to suppress the painful memory of the trade, since to confront it could undermine social cohesion. Some people, therefore, questioned the relevance of teaching the subject and advocate forgetting about it; leaving out that part of history so as to foster unity. He did not agree with this position as he was of the opinion that knowledge cannot hurt but that too little of it can.

Q (i) in Brazil also described his feelings of pain about the TTEA. He said he felt very affected by it and tried to bring feelings to the forefront of the class. Expressing her own concern, another Brazilian teacher, Q (ii), wanted to ensure that slavery trafficking and discrimination, which remain problems in Brazil, would be vanquished. She was interested in social justice.

## ESCAPING A SENSE OF GUILT OR A MYOPIC PERSPECTIVE OF AFRICAN HISTORY

Teacher B in the UK, acknowledging that both black and white students find the subject 'a very powerful, emotive one,' stated that care was taken not to leave students with a sense of guilt or with a myopic appreciation of African history.

## STUDENTS' INTEREST AROUSED AND PERFORMANCE IMPROVED

Teachers in the interview sessions observed a desire on the part of students to discuss their thoughts on the information being shared with them. Teacher I (iii) in Barbados noted the importance of giving students the opportunity to express themselves and allowed her students to do so. Teacher A in London, teaching this subject to students of Caribbean roots also observed her students' need to talk about what they are learning.

Teacher Q (iv) in Brazil noted that being exposed to information about the subject made students interested in learning more about it so they 'go out and do more research.'

H in the Gambia also commented on the interest which the subject aroused in her students and how involved they became. Consequently, they performed better in this area of the curriculum than in others.

# STUDENTS' EMOTIONS

## SADNESS, SORROW, OUTRAGE AND TEARS

Barbadian students involved in the UNESCO Associated Schools 'Transatlantic Slave Trade Education Project' wrote of their feelings and learning experiences within the Project, in preparation for their participation in the European Youth Encounter which was held in Bristol, UK in November, 2000. Some of their written accounts point to their feelings of sadness and sorrow to learn about the terrible experience of the enslaved and the horrible conditions they had to withstand. They commented on their feelings of sorrow and despair that the lives and families of the enslaved had been destroyed. One student said that 'The slave trade was a great tragedy and should have never taken place.'

T (iii) in Trinidad and Tobago referred to the initial outrage which occurs each time she approaches the topic anew. J (i) in Jamaica pointed to the feelings of animosity and anger which the topic could arouse in students, explaining that, sometimes, students vent their feelings by making declarations like, 'I hate all white people and if I was a slave I would have killed them.'

Teacher A in London, teaching students of Caribbean background, said that she sees her students cry and the educator in the Dominican Republic said that he and his students do get emotional about it and cry sometimes. J (iii) in Jamaica explained that if the students see teachers become emotional, they will also become emotional.

## Cannot be Held Responsible or Feel Guilt

Student X, the male student from Denmark, did not agree with one of his female classmates who had earlier stated that she would like to apologize to young people in the Caribbean for the TTEA and that she felt sorry about it. Student X was of the view that while the trade was to be regretted, there should be no question for him of apologizing or feeling sorry as it happened in a past over which he had no influence and was not his fault. He thought this to be the best approach to adopt to avoid feelings of resentment or hatred today and saw communication as being important in promoting this approach. Student Y, a female student, was of a similar view. While she described students as being 'still in shock that something like this could happen' she said they could not go back and change it; that they were not 'the bad guys' because of what their ancestors did and that they could not apologize. While they could certainly try to prevent it from happening again, or try to stop what is happening now, they could not apologise.

The same student, nonetheless, did speak of feeling a sense of guilt, even though Denmark did not play as big a part in the TTEA as did other countries. She found her feelings of guilt, therefore, hard to explain. However, she was surprised by many of the facts she learned. When she thought of slavery, she always thought of 'the blacks working the cotton fields in the United States' and never knew that so many went to Brazil and the Caribbean. There were many things she did not know. She concluded that it was necessary to deal with all these facts and that the TTEA was not something to look back on 'with a lot of pride.'

## STUDENTS' EMOTIONAL RESPONSES TO THE TOPIC OF THE MIDDLE PASSAGE

Teachers in Barbados discussed the considerable emotional response, including horror and disbelief, which the theme of the Middle Passage evoked from their students when they learned of the conditions under which the enslaved Africans were shipped.

Teacher I (i) in Barbados said when her students looked at images of the Middle Passage, they could not believe people could be shipped as the enslaved were: hot, hungry and sick; made to lie in their own faeces, to urinate on each other; to be thrown overboard to be eaten by the waiting sharks. It was as though they could not believe what happened, but when they saw the film *Amistad*, she believed they came to grips with what the conditions were really like on the slave ship.

I (ii) in Barbados recognized two principal reactions in her students: disbelief and horror. Many students said they were sad about what they were learning, while others became angry and were very vocal about what they would have done in that same situation.

From the reaction of teachers in Jamaica when the topic of the Middle Passage was raised (there was a chorus of murmuring, even some laughter), it would appear that this topic was also particularly emotive for their students. Here too teachers spoke of students crying sometimes and becoming emotional. J (i) said students could become exceedingly hostile when the Middle Passage was being taught and when they read about how the enslaved Africans were packed and the conditions of the voyage.

The Middle Passage also evoked great distress among students in the Gambia and the UK. Teacher C in the UK reported that students could not cope with the conditions of the Middle Passage seen on videos. The students ask, 'How did they put up with it?'

Student X in Denmark spoke of being shocked and disturbed by the story of the Middle Passage, especially when he imagined himself in the conditions the enslaved had to endure. It was a story that he would have preferred not to know, and thought that the subject was as emotional for white people as for black people. He declared that it was important to prevent this from happening again and believed it was a good thing to have slavery as part of the history curriculum.

## STUDENTS' RESENTMENT, ANGER, FRUSTRATION AND FASCINATION

Teacher B in the UK also spoke of students' resentment and anger, explaining that in a more general sense, this had to do perhaps, with the injustice of man to man, rather than with a personal identification with the descendants of the TTEA. He explained that he tried to get his class to feel empathy for enslaved Africans and typically the feelings he observed were those of resentment that people could be treated in an inhumane fashion by other human beings.

Teacher C in the UK also noted that his students felt anger about the inhumanity of the trade rather than the racism involved. They simply could not believe that human beings could hurt fellow human beings in such a way.

Administrator 2 in the USA, referring to the book of poetry written by students at the public school in New Orleans involved in the UNESCO Associated Schools 'Transatlantic Slave Trade Education Project', stated that it 'speaks volumes.... You can literally feel the emotions.' The students, he said, were able to meet author Earnest Gaines, who talked about oppression and how black people deal with oppression. They were touched by his discussion.

The main catalyst for these students' emotional release was the visit to Laura Plantation where they viewed the shacks in which the enslaved Africans lived. They were introduced to the horrors of enslavement and life as an enslaved African on a Louisiana cane plantation. They were shown the depths of perdition. When they saw the fine living arrangements that the Europeans enjoyed as opposed to the shacks and the squalor in which the Africans dwelt, all of those things shaped their emotional responses which were anger and sorrow. Some compared their experiences in their community to the experiences of enslaved children and many of them became resolute in their determination to improve their own lives.

F and G in Benin and Senegal respectively noted that, in drawing their students' attention to the human tragedy of the TTEA, they were sometimes confronted with their students' revulsion and even personal animosity as the subject evoked a deep anger. Sometimes students turned their anger against the teacher. Teacher F explained that he is from Abome in the region of Aoyo. The students believed that all the people coming from his region collaborated in some way with the slave traders. They look for his assurance that his family was not involved in the trade and he told them not everyone was responsible for what took place during the TTEA; that not all the people from Abome played a role in it.

Teacher G, in Senegal, also confirmed that, in general, teaching the TTEA arouses deep anger.

T (ii) in Trinidad and Tobago spoke of her students' fascination with the subject; their interest in the experience of the sexual exploitation of the enslaved women and their feelings of general outrage which she felt even if they did not articulate them.

According to SGO in the Dominican Republic, the subject aroused 'lots of anger' among students of European ancestry in his class, as well as a negative response in some of his students of African ancestry. When he asked students of European ancestry why they were so angry they explain that it is because this history had been hidden from them because it was wrong. Most of his students of African history also did not know the history of the trade in the way that he taught it, that is, from an Afrocentric perspective, and some students become very upset.

## Students' Confusion, Disbelief and Horror

Teachers indicated that their students seemed incredulous that a phenomenon such as the TTEA could have occurred. Teacher C in the UK reported his students asking, 'Why didn't they all just turn on the owners?' Teacher E in Denmark stated that some of his students became very emotional and found it incredible that something so horrible could have taken place.

Similarly, in Barbados, students' feelings of anger, hostility and of distress gave way to feelings of confusion and disbelief that the enslaved Africans could not overpower their white captors; that although they outnumbered the Europeans in Africa and in the Caribbean, they did not rise up and take over and resist their enslavement. Some students tended to conclude that the Africans were either weak or stupid and teachers themselves were 'at a loss to explain that except to say that the Europeans had superior weapons,' as one teacher put it. Such an explanation did not satisfy these students who still asked why the enslaved Africans did not resist their capture, knowing that some would have to die. Teachers in turn asked students to place themselves in the situation of the enslaved Africans and to consider the reality of human nature and who would be prepared to die first. This helped to bring students face to face with the difficult reality of accepting certain death even if life meant one under the conditions of slavery.

These comments by students seemed indicative of an inadequate focus by the teachers concerned on the resistance of the enslaved Africans to their enslavement.

## Denial and Lack of Interest on the Part of Students

Teacher A in the UK spoke of the complexity of the emotional response on the part of students of Caribbean background which resulted from her efforts to put into a contemporary context the duration of the TTEA. It was only when she drew to their attention the fact that Africans were not Caribbean indigenous peoples that they begin to understand the impact of the trade. She also highlighted the denial of students of Caribbean roots of their African heritage. They felt they had no roots in Africa and there tended to be 'a massive divide between the African people and the Caribbean people'.

Students of Caribbean heritage expressed no desire to own African culture and ancestry. Another divide that existed among Teacher A's black students was those who found it very hard to learn this history and others who recognized that they were learning something about their history and really wanted to know it.

The students of Caribbean background at the London school and the students interviewed in Jamaica shared a lack of interest, as descendants of Africans, about their past.

In Jamaica, among those students who freely allowed themselves to experience the feelings of sadness and sorrow, joy and pride which learning this history evokes, there were students who did not want to know anything about this past. One male student from Jamaica, Student A, expressed his own sense of being at a loss to understand this lack of interest. He suggested the students' lack of interest might be a result of boredom through the manner in which the subject was taught, that is, lectures without supporting visual aids that might help them to better understand the material.

One Jamaican teacher explained some students' resistance to learning about the subject with the observation that, 'It makes them feel inferior.' This statement was immediately corroborated by Student B who perhaps highlights the degree to which Caribbean youth of African descent can identify strongly with the suffering of the enslaved.

## Students' Awareness of the Legacies of the Transatlantic Trade in Enslaved Africans in Relations Among Blacks and Whites

Both students X and Y in Denmark spoke about their experiences in other countries where they became aware of the legacies of the TTEA, as reflected in race relations and stereotyping of blacks and other minorities. Student X, while on a recent visit to South Africa, found that all the employees at his hotel were black. Seeing them dressed in white doing their job, probably for little money, reminded him of slavery. Student Y, while attending school in the USA in 2001 observed at her school the existing segregation between black and white students. She noted that blacks and Hispanics 'have a lot of people looking down on them' and that the 'black kids talked to the black kids and the white kids talked to the white kids most of the time. That is just how it was.' She also spoke of having to remind herself sometimes 'not to let certain thoughts enter [her] mind' when she sees a black person walking down the street and stated that she feels guilty about noticing somebody through the colour of his or her skin. Student X concluded that there was a continuing need for mutual understanding and that this needs to be developed in future generations but that it would take a long time.

## EMOTIONAL RESPONSES OF NON-AFRICAN STUDENTS IN BARBADOS AND TRINIDAD AND TOBAGO

### Empathy

Barbados is largely a society of people of African origin, with a minority population of the descendants of the wealthy white plantation class, though not all whites in Barbados are wealthy. It is not surprising, therefore, that the Barbadian teachers commented on the responses, or lack thereof, of the white students they taught. The white students were described as being quiet and trying not to show emotion, while the teachers felt uncomfortable and unsure of how to handle the situation; that they wished to take into consideration how white students might feel while presenting the facts of the history of the TTEA. This was particularly challenging when they were accustomed to having predominantly students of African ancestry in their classrooms. When they found that there were also a few students of European ancestry, they were not mentally prepared for teaching them.

In Trinidad and Tobago on the other hand, where the Afro- and Indo-Trinidadian populations are the same size, the questionnaire on the emotional responses of teaching and learning about the TTEA was completed by teachers at a Muslim girls' school with a significant Indo-Trinidadian student body. In spite of the increasing divisiveness of Trinidad and Tobago politics, teachers in this school were able to show empathy with the African experience. One of the teachers of this school indicated that participation in the UNESCO Associated Schools 'Transatlantic Slave Trade Education Project' facilitated 'a better understanding of how the Africans were affected...'. Another teacher at the school commented that participation in the Project proved to be a great asset. The Project encouraged them to adopt an Afrocentric perspective in teaching the subject. They empathized with the Africans, felt anger at the destruction of African civilization, but also felt great pride in the contribution of Africans to the New World.

T (i) in Trinidad and Tobago also had the opportunity to teach the subject to students who were predominantly non-African and observed that like Afro-Trinidadian students, they too could not understand how the TTEA and the exploitation of the human resources of one particular group could have occurred and persisted for so long.

In Trinidad and Tobago, therefore, there was evidence of Indo-Trinidadian students empathizing with the history of enslavement of Afro-Trinidadians.

### Feelings of Pride on Learning of their African Heritage

A review of the written work of Barbadian students preparing to participate in the Youth Forum organized under the umbrella of the UNESCO Project revealed one student's awareness and understanding that it was because of the trade that people of African origin were living in the West Indies. Another student expressed her surprise, astonishment and pride at discovering the contributions of Africans. She wrote:

> I was especially surprised and astonished to find out that the first person to perform an open heart surgery was a Black person and that the person who made the stop lights was also Black. These are great achievements and there are also many more. Although Black persons had a rough and horrible past, they have made many contributions and I am very proud of my African heritage and their creativity.

I (iii) in Barbados, while not noticing any great difference in her students as a result of learning about the subject, did observe that they were happy and proud to learn about their African ancestry and to be in a position to pass on their knowledge to other people.

Student B in Jamaica, expressing some sense of pride in the achievement of Africans, even as she acknowledged that her classmates tend to feel 'little' on learning about the TTEA, explained, 'We'll think about it, then we'll see how far we've come. We've come a very long way and you know we've achieved a lot, so we're proud of it, to some extent.'

Teacher T (iii) in Trinidad and Tobago also reported the impact of the Project on her students' heightened appreciation for and interest in history as well as on their sense of pride. She said that some students remarked quite openly that they were proud to be descendants of enslaved Africans whereas at the beginning of the Project 'they were openly embarrassed at their blackness.'

## AFRICAN AMERICAN STUDENTS' INCREASED CAPACITY FOR EMPATHY

Teacher B in the USA reflected with satisfaction that, as a result of the educational experience of learning about the TTEA, it was possible to see evidence of students' growth in terms of their ability to empathize with others. She commented that they began to look at other people with some level of compassion and understanding and that this was wonderful for their continuing maturity.

## A PERCEPTION OF THE HUMAN TRAGEDY OF THE TRANSATLANTIC TRADE IN ENSLAVED AFRICANS AS CONTINUING TODAY

Teacher I (i) in Barbados commented on the negative relations which may exist today among people of African descent as a legacy of the TTEA. Mental slavery must still be overcome. This idea was also developed in the comments of Teachers I (ii) and I (iii) in Barbados who noted that the positive changes observed in students as a result of their participation in the UNESCO Project appeared temporary or short lived. While students showed the outrage which the subject matter evoked in the classroom, they soon resumed their familiar pattern of speaking to one another disparagingly about being black. This would seem to indicate a need for sustained efforts at addressing the psychological legacies of the TTEA in Caribbean societies.

# TEACHERS' EMOTIONS

## SATISFACTION, ACCOMPLISHMENT, PRIDE, ENJOYMENT

Amidst the emotional turmoil, the ambiguity and uncertainty regarding effective coping strategies and the pedagogical challenge presented by teaching this subject from an emotional perspective, it was very clear that many of the teachers interviewed, or who completed the questionnaire about emotions, derived great satisfaction and even joy from imparting knowledge of this subject to their students. Teacher T (iii) in Trinidad and Tobago, for example, declared that she was happy and proud to have chosen the profession of teaching.

The pattern of commentary by teachers in Trinidad and Tobago, Jamaica and the UK reflects the sense of satisfaction that these teachers derived from passing on knowledge of the history of the TTEA. In Trinidad and Tobago, one teacher wrote of 'feeling a sense of accomplishment, motivation when students begin to enquire about certain issues and discussions take place.' Another teacher initially felt a sense of sorrow and resentment at the slave-owners, this was followed by a sense of pride at the great achievement of Africans and their descendants in the New World.

Yet another teacher in Trinidad and Tobago expressed the view that teaching the subject stirred 'a feeling of enjoyment.' This teacher described the experience as 'enlightening and enjoyable', since it provided an opportunity to pass on information and to engage in discussion. Teacher T (i) in Trinidad and Tobago admitted to feelings of confusion since, while he tended to feel anger and hurt about the TTEA, he nonetheless enjoyed teaching the subject. He saw himself 'as an instrument to pass on the information…' and over the years developed his ability to do so.

Teacher J (i) in Jamaica spoke of efforts to look at the positive aspects of the legacies of the trade. She and her colleagues tended to examine the contribution that Africans and their descendants have made. Although they were so oppressed, their culture still lives on, so they look at the positives: what the enslaved Africans brought, what they introduced and what we still have.

The enjoyment and satisfaction derived from teaching the TTEA was also articulated by teachers in the UK. One of these teachers communicated his sense of 'enjoyment that others can share in learning from past mistakes,' and was especially happy to be able to make the subject accessible to young people. Yet another teacher in the UK indicated his sense of satisfaction in teaching the subject matter, his pride in his colleagues and also his respect for the enslaved, for their triumph in adversity and their resilience in difficult circumstances.

## SOME INSIGHTS SHARED BY TEACHERS ON STRATEGIES TO COPE WITH THE EMOTIONAL DIMENSION OF TEACHING THE TRANSATLANTIC TRADE IN ENSLAVED AFRICANS

Teachers shared their insights based on their experiences, regarding strategies which can be effective in dealing with the emotional dimension of teaching and learning about the TTEA in the classroom setting. These strategies included raising the discussion to a higher level; providing students with avenues to express their emotions; guiding them through their emotions; focusing on the resistance of enslaved Africans and on their capacity to overcome; and validating students' feelings.

### RAISING THE DISCUSSION TO A HIGHER LEVEL

Teacher E in Denmark encouraged his students to make informed comments and did not judge them. He explained that he tried to raise the discussion to a higher level all the time. He let his students know that it was acceptable to have different points of view and to espouse them based on increasing knowledge.

### PROVIDING AVENUES TO EXPRESS FEELINGS

Teacher S in the USA spoke of the approaches used to deal with her students' feelings of hurt, anger and pain evoked when they watched the film *Amistad*. She observed that such emotions were evoked even in the young men who 'at this age...dare not show any emotion.' The teachers at this school sought to deal with this by providing their students with avenues to express their feelings. Teachers facilitated students' writing and talking about their emotions to be able to vent their anger.

Teacher I (i) in Barbados was of the view that regardless of the feelings of the teacher, students needed to be provided with the opportunity to express themselves.

## Focusing on Strength of Enslaved Africans and their Capacity to Overcome; Validating Students' Feelings

In trying to guide students through their feelings, Teacher S in the USA explained that they focused on the strength of the enslaved Africans and their capacity to overcome. They also validated the students' feelings of anger. Teachers R and S emphasized that the enslaved Africans did not complacently accept their fate but tried to resist and run away; that the enslaved Africans were angry and that it was all right for students to be angry too.

At the same time, they promoted the idea of the students having personal responsibility, as members of the human race, to ensure that this history was not repeated, even though their own life histories may not allow them the luxury of such thoughts.

Teacher T (iii) in Trinidad and Tobago pointed to the need for teachers to understand that students' emotional responses to the subject should be viewed as a natural part of their emotional development when dealing with human rights and prejudice issues. Teachers must understand that part of what they have to do is to guide students through these emotions. He referred to William Cross's *Model of Racial Identity Development* as being useful in this regard.

## Promoting Intercultural Dialogue

Teacher F in Benin took the position that this is the time for a culture of peace and a culture of tolerance. He was of the view that, in dealing with the TTEA, intercultural dialogue was needed above all else.

# Summary

Teachers in all regions acknowledged the TTEA as an emotive subject and were keenly attuned to their students' emotional responses. Teachers in Barbados, Jamaica and the Gambia, all female, were particularly focused on the need to be balanced and objective in teaching the subject. One male teacher in the UK adopted a 'clinical approach' to the subject.

Teachers observed in their students emotions such as sadness, sorrow and outrage, resulting in tears, as testified by teachers in the

UK, Barbados, Jamaica, Trinidad and Tobago, and the Dominican Republic. In the UK some students' feelings of resentment and anger were said to be linked to their concerns about injustice and inhumanity rather than with a personal identification with the enslaved Africans, or with the racism involved in the trade. In the USA, students' emotional responses of anger and sorrow were described as making them resolute to improve their own lives.

Feelings of pain experienced by both teachers and students were discussed by teachers in the USA, Brazil, and Trinidad and Tobago.

Some students in the UK, Denmark and Barbados, according to their teachers, expressed confusion, disbelief and horror that a phenomenon such as the TTEA could have occurred. However, in the UK and Jamaica, there were also students who manifested a lack of interest in the subject and denial of their African heritage, while in Jamaica some students experienced feelings of inferiority and expressed boredom with history because of the teaching methods.

Not all of the emotions experienced by teachers and students were negative. Some students in Barbados, and Trinidad and Tobago felt a sense of pride on learning about their African heritage. Teachers in Brazil, the Gambia, the UK, and Trinidad and Tobago commented on the interest which the subject aroused in their students, stimulating their desire to talk and, in the case of the Gambia, resulting in increased learning. Students in Trinidad and Tobago were said to have manifested a heightened interest in history.

Students in the USA were described as developing an increased capacity for empathy with others. In the case of Trinidad and Tobago, Indo-Trinidadian teachers and students empathized with the history of enslavement of Afro-Trinidadians.

Teachers in the UK, Jamaica, and Trinidad and Tobago expressed a sense of satisfaction with teaching the subject. However, this feeling of satisfaction also resulted in a sense of confusion within one Trinidad and Tobago teacher since the subject caused him pain and made him angry.

Teaching methodologies employed were seen as affecting students' emotional responses and, in particular, visits to places of memory were viewed as enabling students to establish a personal link with the history of the TTEA.

Teachers from Benin, Barbados, Denmark, USA, and Trinidad and Tobago referred to some strategies used to cope with their students' emotional responses to learning about this history. These included encouraging students to develop their points of view based on knowledge; providing students with avenues to express their feelings and validating these feelings and guiding students through their emotions; focusing on the strengths of the enslaved Africans, the fact that they resisted their enslavement and their capacity to overcome; and encouraging dialogue amongst the descendants of all those who were involved in the TTEA.

Chapter 6 has discussed the emotional dimensions of the pedagogical content knowledge of the teachers in this inquiry. It has also presented data from a few students of their own understandings of their emotional responses to content knowledge of the subject. These insights and understandings are useful in facilitating a fuller appreciation of the complexity of teaching an emotive subject such as this one. They can inform approaches to teacher education, particularly with respect to exploring strategies to successfully manage students' emotions evoked by the subject in the classroom setting. What this chapter has presented are the insights of a small group of teachers and there remains a considerable amount of work to be done in the further understanding of these issues to ensure that teaching the TTEA becomes an empowering experience for all teachers and students. The effective management of emotions must be seen as a very important dimension to teaching this subject so as to contribute to students' understanding of themselves, their self-discovery and their human development.

Chapter 7

# Educational Significance

Chapter 7 discusses the educational significance of the findings of the study into selected teachers' pedagogical content knowledge of the TTEA. The conceptual framework outlined in Chapter 2 informs the discussion

## Insights for Teaching the Transatlantic Trade in Enslaved Africans

### Comprehension: Teachers' Lack of Knowledge

Given that a teacher's knowledge base can be considered the first key input for comprehension, it is noteworthy that throughout the inquiry reported in this book, some teachers referred to their lack of knowledge of particular areas of content knowledge of the TTEA. This lack of knowledge must, therefore, be seen as having a negative impact on expertise for teaching this subject since teacher confidence and expertise come with knowledge and the requisite pedagogical skills, backed up by appropriate teaching materials. Teachers' confidence and expertise are essential to the quality of students' learning alongside other principles such as an understanding of how students learn.

### Transformation: Teachers Transform Content Knowledge of the Transatlantic Trade in Enslaved Africans

Several teachers stood out in their efforts to transform their content knowledge of the subject of the TTEA through their pedagogy, to create a positive impact on the minds and lives of their students, in the interest of their personal enrichment and development. Stimulating students' critical thinking, building empathy and encouraging their creative expression were some of the strategies employed to this end.

## PREPARATION: CRITICAL INTERPRETATION

A few teachers spoke of their efforts at deconstructing the subject matter; as it meant being radical they needed information that was relevant but not overwhelming in volume. This process engaged these teachers in preparation or the critical interpretation of the given text materials, the first process involved in transformation as presented by Shulman (1987). Elements of interpretation, critical analysis and structuring which were evident in teachers' narratives included identifying themes and concepts for teaching the TTEA and the identification of the purposes behind these themes and concepts. For example, the use of nomenclature (enslaved vs slave) was used to 'disempower the enslaver' and to use a more humane reference to enslaved Africans. While such preparation is likely to involve some degree of planning on the part of the selected teachers, they did not make much mention of their preparation in terms of lesson planning, for example. Rather, they tended to focus on specific issues relating to organization of their teaching (which is a dimension of planning) and interaction with their students.

## REPRESENTATION

A second process involved in transformation is that of representing ideas using new analogies and metaphors. Representation engages the teacher in thinking through the main ideas of the text or lesson and finding alternative ways of representing them to students. There was evidence of teachers in the UK and the USA, for example, engaging in this process by organizing their teaching around themes which could be conveniently incorporated into the official curriculum which, as structured, did not allow much opportunity for teaching the TTEA.

Where the structure of the curriculum did include teaching the subject, as in the case of the English-speaking Caribbean, teachers in Barbados, for example, reported teaching using an Afrocentric perspective, also indicative of pedagogical reasoning based on transformation. The representation or re-interpretation of content knowledge of the TTEA from an Afrocentric perspective was intended to adapt content knowledge of the subject to students' general characteristics and needs.

## SELECTION

Chapter 5 discussed strategies used by the teachers interviewed to teach the TTEA. The chapter also discussed the strategies which teachers found to be most successful. These strategies are indicative of these teachers' repertoire of teaching approaches and they reflect instructional methods known to be used by expert teachers as indicated by Shulman. Selection of teaching strategies is an element of Shulman's model.

## ADAPTATION AND TAILORING TO STUDENT CHARACTERISTICS: TEACHING MATERIALS, TEACHING APPROACHES

Teachers in Barbados and the UK were concerned about finding materials at a reading level suited to their students. In the UK teachers had to incur additional costs of money and time in an effort to tailor teaching materials to their students' characteristics.

Most of the teachers, in varying degrees, showed evidence of having engaged in tailoring their teaching to cater to the specific characteristics of their students. This was evident in their:

(i) identifying strategies to link teaching the TTEA to students' current realities;
(ii) sensitizing students, through culture, to respect and value blacks;
(iii) emphasizing the involvement of whites in the anti-slavery movement so that students would not think that all whites were wicked;
(iv) drawing a parallel between the TTEA and the drug trade, described as being evident in the surrounding school community.

It would appear that, in the case of the latter strategy, efforts at adaptation and tailoring overlap with representation mentioned above, given the use of the analogy between the slave trade and the drug trade.

These processes of preparation, representation, selection and adaptation, and tailoring to student characteristics described above, are involved in transformation, an element of pedagogical reasoning and action, as described by Shulman. They inform a plan or set of strategies for the presentation of a lesson, unit or course, and are reflected in these teachers' approaches to teaching the TTEA.

## Instruction: the Challenge of the Multidisciplinary Approach

Teachers employed a range of instructional strategies to facilitate their students' learning and development. These included:

(i) presenting students with different perspectives on an issue and then encouraging them to present their own point of view;

(ii) engaging students in research to enable them to discover something for themselves;

(iii) group work;

(iv) questioning, discovery and inquiry: turning around the story of the TTEA and starting to tell it from the perspective of the enslaved Africans;

(v) teaching students to learn to use a variety of sources and to refer to sources to support their points of view;

(vi) promoting students' creativity and artistic expression;

(vii) the development of a special curriculum, infused into the regular curriculum, to guide teachers in their classroom instruction, without the use of textbooks;

(viii) setting aside a particular day to teach the TTEA using the curriculum mentioned in (vii) above;

(ix) using the regenerative power of the spoken word through guest speakers;

(x) engaging students in journal writing with the support of an academic.

The range of methods of instruction used by these teachers, as well as the variety of subjects through which attempts have been made to teach this topic, are indicative of the methodology of the multidisciplinary approach. However, it was not evident that teachers had mastered the pedagogy of multidisciplinary teaching.

A multidisciplinary approach gathers several disciplines around a theme, idea or concept, with no attempt to integrate them. It requires planning as it involves teamwork among teachers. Teachers must be familiar with and employ a variety of strategies to sustain students' interest, as well as to cater to their diverse needs and abilities. Teaching strategies are dependent upon aims and objectives of teaching (Melville-Myers, 2001). One very experienced teacher identified teaching from a multidisciplinary perspective as his greatest challenge and this seems an important area to be integrated into workshops and seminars which address teachers' professional development related to teaching the TTEA.

## RESOURCES TO SUPPORT INSTRUCTION

Textbooks were not the only source of teachers' content knowledge of the TTEA. As indicated in Chapter 5, teachers also had access to a variety of other sources of content knowledge. Indeed, a few preferred not to use textbooks at all and several considered existing textbooks not quite appropriate to the needs of their students.

Significant use was made of film, videos, pictures, maps and places of memory. Some use was made of CD-ROMS, Internet sources and PowerPoint presentations. Multiple text and technology sources were employed. Teachers spoke of the need for more resources to support instruction. These included: 'more voices of people who fought against the slave trade,' and especially more voices of women: 'the remnants, the artefacts associated with slavery'; textbooks and technological resources appropriate for lower and average ability students; visual resources and larger quantities of relevant and appropriate materials. The production of the kind and quantities of resources which seem to be in demand is an issue to be considered seriously in terms of the allocation of funding and the identification of educators with the requisite skills for the production of such resources.

## Reflection

Instances of teachers engaging in reflection were evident in their articulation of the challenges of teaching the TTEA. Individual teachers reflected on different issues. These included: contradictions arising out of their socialization — a self-image fostered by the experience of slavery and its continued angst. They reflected on their efforts to be as comprehensive as possible in their teaching, in the limited time available; to have their students understand key concepts, and on the need for the opportunity and time to meet and reflect with other teachers about their teaching. They were aware of their own lack of knowledge and the need, therefore, to upgrade their knowledge of the history of the TTEA to enable their students to arrive at a deeper understanding of the subject, within a certain amount of time. They wanted to be able to teach successfully using an interdisciplinary approach and to motivate male students in particular. They lamented the loss of teaching time when they have to re-work material to make it more attractive to students but recognized the importance of changing students' perceptions of Africa and establishing the relevance of teaching the TTEA. Indeed, many of the challenges identified by teachers reflected issues which directly concerned their own teaching such as their knowledge base. They seemed to accept it as their personal responsibility to address this. This is particularly important given the paucity of information available for schools, issues relating to the ideological slant of the knowledge and the challenges of sustaining that knowledge in school contexts.

These teachers also reflected on the need to give their students certain dispositions to be able to treat with the familiar and the unfamiliar. They reflected on issues relating to students' identity formation; their recognition and celebration of different cultures. They were sensitive to students' feelings of shame, guilt and denial of the history of the TTEA and its legacies, and in a few cases even to students' feelings of hostility provoked by this history. They were of the view that education about the TTEA, if effective, could help their students to overcome these feelings. They recognized that in teaching the subject, they needed to manage a set of contradictory voices and to understand what needs to be done to challenge attitudes of mind.

Shulman's Model of Pedagogical Reasoning and Action facilitates a fairly in-depth understanding of teachers' practice and the emerging issues in relation to teaching the TTEA. Given the context of these findings, that is, based on an international UNESCO project and an inquiry that is transatlantic involving three different regional sites across the globe, there are many instances of good teaching practice which can be built upon to develop teacher education curricula for teaching the TTEA. The findings regarding these selected teachers' needs to be able to teach the subject more effectively can also inform teacher education curricula for the professional development of other teachers to teach the TTEA. Such curricula must also treat with issues relating to how students learn. These issues include understanding students' misconceptions about the subject. While it may appear that teachers are making a difference, in fact, students may be doing no more than assimilating what teachers say into the preconceptions they bring with them to the classroom. Another issue involves providing students with a solid foundation of factual knowledge, ordered around the key concepts and thematic areas of the subject to be able to learn.

(Peter J. Leen in M.Suzanne Donovan and John D. Bransford, eds, 2005, 31-32).

## THE EMOTIONAL DIMENSION OF TEACHERS' PEDAGOGICAL CONTENT KNOWLEDGE OF THE TRANSATLANTIC TRADE IN ENSLAVED AFRICANS

The responses of teachers interviewed confirm the affirmation of Rosiek (2003) and McCaughtry (2004) that human experience is emotional since, in all three regions constituting this multi-site case study, almost all of the teachers acknowledged the TTEA as an emotive subject.

That the teachers were keenly attuned to their students' emotional responses supports the finding of McCaughtry that teachers' understanding of emotion in the classroom is an integral part of their pedagogical content knowledge. Anticipation of students' emotions which might have been discomforting in the classroom context seemed to have influenced teachers' decision making. Some teachers were concerned with trying to reduce unconstructive emotions, such as prejudice or bias against whites that might inhibit students' appreciation of the fact that whites were also very instrumental in abolishing the TTEA or that Africans themselves sold their own people into slavery.

Several teachers commented that the subject stimulated their students' desire to talk, an indication that they were very likely listening to their students and in tune with their feelings. This is a finding also reported by McCaughtry (2004) in his research involving an experienced teacher who demonstrated a high level of emotional understanding.

Teachers' descriptions of students desire to talk, and of their emotions including sadness, sorrow, anger and outrage, on learning about the TTEA, reflect Goleman's (1995) families of emotions and validate Dewey's (1931/1980) tenet that education takes place when ideas and knowledge are translated into emotion, interest and volition.

As reported by Tatum (1992), discomfort, avoidance, denial and guilt are some common human reactions to race-related subject matter. Teachers in this study commented on how hard the subject of the TTEA was to teach, how difficult to handle. The importance of context in understanding emotion in the classroom was highlighted with the explanation that the subject was particularly hard to teach when white teachers taught black students who might feel they were learning something negative about themselves. This enlightening observation highlighted the perspective that as the victims of the TTEA, blacks were likely to continue to be victims as they were the ones expected to be more psychologically oppressed by this history. Nonetheless, in the Caribbean context, teachers did report the discomfort of white students on being taught the subject by black teachers and their own uncertainty about how to deal with their white students' discomfort. Black students were also said to be inclined to deny their African heritage and there were reports of students' feelings of inferiority. Rosiek (2003) indicates that unconstructive emotions inhibit students' learning. Teachers, therefore, need to be trained to respond appropriately to such feelings if their teaching is to have a positive impact on their students' development. Students' self-image must be seen as a critical component of their personal development. Teaching methodology was said to impact upon students' emotions; students becoming more emotionally engaged when visiting Places of Memory. Such emotional experiences were seen as facilitating student learning. It was reported, however, that not possessing the skills to handle students' emotions in the classroom, some teachers avoided teaching the subject out of fear of a backlash.

Students' emotional responses to the topic of the Middle Passage in particular were illustrative of their sharing vicariously the feelings of the enslaved Africans on board the slave ship. Denzin (1984) identifies the sharing of feelings vicariously and being able to empathize with others, even when there are no similar experiences, as one means of inter-subjective emotional understanding.

Students' constructive emotional responses, such as feelings of pride, sparked their interest in the subject and facilitated their learning. These emotions of students, their heightened interest in the subject matter of the TTEA and their increased learning had as a parallel teachers' own constructive emotions and their increased sense of satisfaction, accomplishment, motivation and enjoyment in relation to teaching the subject. The complexity of the emotions of students and teachers alike points to the importance of the context of teaching in relation to teachers' own emotion in the classroom, and underscores the concern of Rosiek (2003) that care must be taken not to oversimplify the issue of classroom emotion. While the interviews with teachers did not explicitly explore the issue of emotional scaffolding as elaborated by Rosiek, teachers nonetheless did provide some evidence of this, as reflected in the insights they shared regarding ways of coping with the emotional dimension of teaching the TTEA. As explained by Rosiek, the term *scaffolding,* traced to Vygotsky's (1997) *Social Psychology*, concerns teachers' strategies for assisting their students in cognitively framing their learning experience. Scaffolding aimed at influencing students' *emotional* response to an idea is termed *emotional scaffolding.*

Implicit approaches to emotional scaffolding, as indicated by teachers' attempts to foster students' constructive emotions in relation to the TTEA were:

(i) raising discussions of the subject to 'a higher level';
(ii) providing students with avenues to express their emotions; and
(iii) focusing on the resistance of enslaved Africans and their capacity to overcome suffering.

Explicit or more direct approaches to elicit students' constructive emotions were:

(i) taking students to places of memory to stimulate their interest, their learning and to build empathy
(ii) guiding students through their emotions.

Teachers' implicit approaches to emotional scaffolding, so as to reduce their students' unconstructive emotions when learning about the TTEA, were as follows:

(i) teachers focusing on being balanced and objective in their teaching;
(ii) adopting a clinical approach to the subject;
(iii) encouraging students to develop their point of view based on knowledge
(iv) 'de-dramatizing' the TTEA.

There was no evidence of teachers' explicit attempts to reduce students' unconstructive emotions about the subject. These approaches by teachers to emotional scaffolding are presented in Table 1 based on Rosiek's (2003) emotional scaffolding typology.

## Table 1
## Indications of Implicit and Explicit Emotional Scaffolding Employed by Teachers in Teaching the TTEA

| Approach to Emotional Scaffolding | Attempts to Foster Constructive Emotions about the TTEA | Attempts to Reduce Unconstructive Emotions about the TTEA |
|---|---|---|
| Implicit | <ul><li>Raising discussions to a higher level (Teacher E, Denmark)</li><li>Providing students with avenues to express their emotions (Barbados, Trinidad and Tobago, USA)</li><li>Focusing on the resistance of enslaved Africans and their capacity to overcome trials (USA)</li></ul> | <ul><li>Teachers focused on being balanced and objective (Barbados, Jamaica, the Gambia)</li><li>Clinical approach to the subject (UK)</li><li>Encouraging students to develop their points of view, based on knowledge (Teacher A, Trinidad and Tobago)</li><li>De-dramatizing the subject (Benin)</li></ul> |
| Explicit | <ul><li>Taking students to places of memory to stimulate their interest and learning through feelings and building empathy (Benin, Brazil, Trinidad and Tobago, USA)</li><li>Guiding students through their emotions (Teacher (iii), Trinidad and Tobago)</li></ul> | |

## Teaching the Transatlantic Trade in Enslaved Africans:

### *The Reformed Vision of Curriculum and Human Development*

The findings of the study are also relevant to elements of Shepard's (2000) observations about the cognitive revolution and the reformed vision of the curriculum. These elements are: the concept of the mind; learning as active mental construction and sense making; the function of emotional filters; self-monitoring and awareness; and teacher expertise. Other manifestations of the reformed vision of the curriculum are also discussed.

## The Concept of the Mind

Shepard's observations about the reformed vision of the curriculum are applicable to teaching the TTEA. The historiography of the TTEA is challenging subject matter given the breadth of its content knowledge, the on going debates surrounding some key issues and the diversity of interpretations of that knowledge in the Americas/ Caribbean, Africa and Europe. The development of students' minds, for example, in developing their critical thinking skills to acquire an in-depth understanding of the subject and its relevance to their lives and to the contemporary world is important and valuable.

## Learning as Active Mental Construction and Sense Making

Teaching the TTEA engages students in asking questions, going beyond the texts, images, and illustrations presented to them to seek to uncover other clues which can inform learning. It engages students in checking various sources and different kinds of sources as a means of learning. These processes are not mechanistic but oriented towards inquiry and discovery. They are skills that enhance students' capacity for learning to know as an essential aspect of their ongoing human development.

## The Function of Emotional Filters

The earlier discussion on the emotional dimension of selected teachers' pedagogical content knowledge of the TTEA is illustrative of the importance of the acknowledgement, in the reformed vision of the curriculum of the function of emotional filters in either enabling or impeding learning. Such filters can be viewed as part of the inner journey leading to the maturing of the personality and learning to be. If, in the process of navigating the turbulent emotions which can be generated by content knowledge of the TTEA, teachers and students emerge with renewed self-respect, and indeed respect for human dignity, it is possible that teaching and learning about the subject would have contributed to enhancing the quality of life for those concerned.

## SELF-MONITORING AND AWARENESS

Shepard's observation about the cognitive revolution appears to parallel the concept of pedagogical content knowledge which promotes the idea that good teaching reflects the intersection of knowledge and effective pedagogy. In this inquiry, teachers, in their narratives, often revealed this intersection in their own experience, since they were frequently sharing with the author not only the content knowledge they were teaching but, inevitably, the ways in which they approached their teaching to facilitate students' learning and human development. This is indicative of their ongoing self-monitoring and awareness, a process which parallels Shulman's process of reflection as an element in teachers' reasoning and action.

## TEACHER EXPERTISE

The reformed vision of the curriculum calls for a principled and coherent way of thinking and representing problems, as opposed to accumulation of information, thus constituting 'expertise' in a field of study. Here again, there appears to be a parallel between Shepard's reformed vision of the curriculum and Shulman's Model of Pedagogical Reasoning and Action in relation to teachers' approaches to teaching the TTEA. For Shulman, teacher expertise should have an intellectual basis which can be informed by an emphasis on pedagogical content knowledge in teacher education curricula.

All of the teachers, in their narratives, provided evidence of principled and coherent thinking in their approaches to teaching the subject. However, they seemed to possess varying degrees of an intellectual basis for teaching it and therefore the level of expertise in evidence seemed to vary. The highest level of expertise in evidence was not limited to the English-speaking Caribbean where the subject is an integral part of the formal secondary school history curriculum, and where teachers seemed to have greater levels of content knowledge. Rather teachers functioning in educational contexts where the TTEA was not a formal part of the secondary school curriculum, notably in the USA, and to a certain extent in the UK, showed evidence of high levels of pedagogical content knowledge and thus expertise, where they were confident in teaching specific aspects of content knowledge. In these cases, teachers' expertise was also evident in their pedagogical skills in adapting content knowledge to their students' characteristics.

## OTHER MANIFESTATIONS OF THE REFORMED VISION OF THE CURRICULUM

Other dimensions of Shepard's (2000) reformed vision of curriculum, evident in the findings of the study, are: the importance of the social and cultural context for learning; the impact of the affective and socially supported interactions on the development of cognitive abilities; and the ways in which social mediation also shapes identity.

The reformed vision of the curriculum promotes, as a key principle, the ability of all students to learn. Several teachers in this study have indirectly endorsed this principle in their calls for the right kinds of learning materials on the TTEA to accommodate students at different levels of ability. These calls seem to be indicative of teachers' beliefs that the support of appropriate pedagogical tools is essential so that all of their students can indeed learn. The reformed vision of the curriculum also calls for equal opportunity for diverse learners. This requires providing genuine opportunities for high-quality instruction and interfacing with academic curricula, consistent with home and community language and interaction patterns.

The importance of the link between the school and the world outside is also underscored in the reformed vision of curriculum. To the extent that teachers were exposing their students to guest speakers, new information communication technologies, places of memory, and even travel abroad programmes, they were also implementing the reformed vision of curriculum. The relevance of this is not only to make learning more interesting and motivating to students, but also to develop their ability to use knowledge in real-world settings. Such experience encourages students in learning to do — another essential dimension of their continuing human development.

In addition to developing cognitive skills, the reformed vision of curriculum also seeks to instill in students important dispositions such as a willingness to continue to try to solve difficult problems. Through these selected teachers' pedagogical content knowledge of the TTEA, their students were engaged in thinking about a phenomenon in history with very real legacies in the modern world. These legacies pose many difficult societal problems at various levels of daily existence. Knowledge of the history of the TTEA and an understanding of its legacies not only highlight the challenges of learning to live together but can also assist students in identifying solutions to the resulting contemporary challenges, particularly where their own human development is concerned.

## RECOMMENDATIONS

1. The strengthening of teacher knowledge must be seen as an on going process in teachers' professional development, both self-initiated and facilitated by the relevant educational authorities. Sharing of teaching experiences, collaboration with educators in formal and non-formal settings and opportunities for travel must all be embraced within this process of teachers' ongoing professional development in pursuit of comprehension and mastery of the subject of the TTEA. Ultimately, teachers' professional development should seek to ensure their commitment to improving and advancing their knowledge and being able to organize it through learning experiences for students. Competent teacher development requires a focus on teachers' skills, their knowledge of how to improve those skills and a commitment to the enhancement and use of their knowledge in collaborative and transformational ways.
2. In addition to the deepening of content knowledge of the TTEA, professional development of teachers should serve to develop their capacity to engage in the processes of Shulman's Model of Pedagogical Reasoning and Action to ensure their preparation for teaching the subject with the highest level of pedagogical expertise. This is important as a means of ensuring that teaching this subject provides students not only with content knowledge but also with skills supportive of their human development.
3. Teachers should be encouraged to engage in documentation, analysis and discussion. Such activity can help to produce

teachers who are thoughtful, innovative and research oriented and who, consequently, can establish for their students a more relevant and appropriate set of learning experiences to facilitate new comprehension about the history of the TTEA and its significance to their lives.

4. Teachers' pedagogical content knowledge for teaching the TTEA from a multidisciplinary perspective should be assessed to identify specific skill areas in need of strengthening.

5. The production of varied types of teaching resources at the required pedagogical levels, and in sufficient quantities must remain an area of priority; a priority that parallels that of ongoing professional development of teachers. In particular, secondary school textbooks should cater to students of average ability who make up the majority of secondary school population.

6. There is need for variety in teaching materials not just in form but also in treatment of content knowledge, organization and presentation. Further, variety should be reflected in the ways in which teachers package and organize teaching materials in different socio-cultural contexts. Teachers, therefore, need access to the process by which historians generate texts and other teaching materials so that they understand the historians' values and orientation. This should allow for teachers to engage more critically with teaching materials.

7. The production of texts and other teaching materials should involve teachers and the mentoring of teachers should be part of this effort. Teachers should be trained in the evaluation, design and production of materials for classroom use in different socio-cultural contexts.

8. There is need to develop clearer understanding about the demands which the emotional dimensions of teaching the TTEA place on teachers and their students.

CHAPTER 8

# CONCLUSION

This book has reported on a qualitative multi-site case study into selected teachers' pedagogical content knowledge of the TTEA. The wider context of the study was the UNESCO Associated Schools 'Transatlantic Slave Trade Education Project' conducted in three geographic regions: Africa, the Americas and the Caribbean, and Europe. The principal interviewees, secondary school teachers, came from very diverse socioeconomic and cultural contexts, and educational systems. These differences, however, did not appear to produce rigid distinctions which set teachers in one region apart from those in another, as the experience of teaching seemed to be dependent on some common factors across the regions. An educational system which attributed importance and value to teaching the TTEA; the knowledge, understanding and pedagogical competencies of the teacher in relation to this subject; and effective teaching materials all affected the relative success or failure of teachers' ability to handle teaching the TTEA. The pedagogical content knowledge of the teachers investigated in this study, their mirroring of several of the elements of the reformed vision of the curriculum and the potential for education about the TTEA to contribute to human development can prove to be invaluable for an in-depth appreciation of the factors at play in teaching the TTEA. The findings of the study, therefore, can inform the development of teacher education curricula for teaching the TTEA.

Teaching the TTEA is important since education for peace and sustainable human development relies on improving shared understandings. One of the major ways of doing this is confronting, and learning from, phenomena in human affairs that violate the principles of human development.

Walvin (2001) identifies factors which contribute to the subject of the TTEA finding a niche in contemporary public memory. In Europe, sections of the public are now very interested in seeking redress, explanation or truth-telling about this brutal aspect of Europe's recent history. The shift in public perception in Europe can also be explained by the presence of the offspring of West Indian immigrants from the postcolonial, post-1945 period. This generation of black Europeans is now demanding a different kind of history one which properly recognizes formerly oppressed peoples, as well as the relationship between European colonialism and Africa. Further, people in Africa, Asia and the Americas, formerly subject to colonialism, have begun the project of rewriting their own history; discarding Eurocentric approaches and values which previously shaped historical interpretations.

The reparations debate is certain to give greater prominence to the history of the TTEA and highlight the relevance of teaching the subject. As UNESCO has recognized through its initiatives under the umbrella of the Slave Route Project, quality education about the TTEA is one attempt at beginning the process towards full reparation. If through teaching the subject, the descendants of those who enslaved Africans for the purpose of the trade can acknowledge the debt owed its contemporary victims, if memory can be purified, black self-esteem rebuilt and the values consistent with a genuine commitment to human development universally pursued and upheld, then the field of education would have contributed significantly to the pursuit of reparations for the past wrongs of the TTEA. Goulbourne (2001) warns, however, that European civilization and the African diaspora will always have to live with the deep scar of the Transatlantic Trade in Enslaved Africans, as it cannot be compensated for by one or two commemorations. Robinson (2001) asserts additionally that blacks will have to heal their spirits for the most part on their own. These are observations which must be taken very seriously by educators in Africa and in the African diaspora in particular. Educational leaders must accept the responsibility, as adults and caregivers, to address the healing of the psyches of black youths, by enlightening them about the violations wrought against their ancestors; their own experience of the legacies of these violations; and especially the lessons of survival and triumph of the human spirit which stand out as beacons for them and for future generations.

# Select Bibliography

Abdul, R. N. 2000. "Thoughts on the Atlantic slave trade: The roles of Africans and the issue of apology for slavery." *West Africa Review.* Retrieved November 11, 2000 from: *www.westafricareview.com/war/vol1.2/vol1.2a/NaAllah.html*

Aidoo, A. A. 2001. "Of forts, castles, and silences." In G. Oostindie (Ed.), *Facing up to the past: Perspectives on the commemoration of slavery from Africa, the Americas and Europe*: 29-34. Kingston, Jamaica: Ian Randle Publishers.

Amagi, I. 1996. "Upgrading the quality of school education." In *Learning: The Treasure Within. Report to UNESCO of the International Commission on Education for the Twenty-first Century*: 199-200. Paris: UNESCO.

Austen, R. A. 2001. "The slave trade as history and memory: Confrontations of slave voyage documents and communal traditions." *The William and Mary Quarterly,* 58 (1): 229-244.

Baba K. I. 2001. "Popularisation of the history of the slave trade." In D. Dične (Ed.), *From chains to bonds: The slave trade revisited*: xxii-xxv. Paris: UNESCO.

Bacchus, M.K. 1979. "Education as a social control mechanism." *The Alberta Journal of Educational Research, XXV* (3): 160-173.

Bailyn, B. 2001. "Considering the slave trade: History and memory." *The William and Mary Quarterly,* 58 (1), 245-251.

Bales, K. 2000. *Disposable people: New slavery in the global economy.* London: University of California Press.

Beckles, H. 2003 *Slave Voyages: The Transatlantic Trade in Enslaved Africans.* Paris: UNESCO

Beckles, H. McD. and V. Shepherd (Eds.) 2002. *Slave voices: The sounds of freedom.* Paris: UNESCO.

Beckles, H. McD. 2001. "Emancipation in the British Caribbean." In G. Oostindie (Ed.), *Facing up to the past: Perspectives on the commemoration of slavery from Africa, the Americas and Europe*: 90-94. Kingston, Jamaica: Ian Randle Publishers.

Beckles, H. McD 2000. "UNESCO Associated Schools Project Network (ASPnet) schools' history questionnaire: The transatlantic slave trade." *Report on Responses*. Mona, Jamaica: The University of the West Indies.

Best, L. 2003, June, 14. "The Afro-Saxon heritage." *Trinidad Express*, 11.

Blackburn, R. 1999. *The making of new world slavery: From the baroque to the modern 1492-1800*. London: Verso.

Blakely, A. 2001. "Remembering slavery in the United States." In G. Oostindie (Ed.), *Facing up to the past: Perspectives on the commemoration of slavery from Africa, the Americas and Europe*: 90-94. Kingston, Jamaica: Ian Randle Publishers.

Buttenschon, C. and P. F. Statens 2002 (Eds.). *Transatlantic Slave Trade Education Project, Denmark: Annual Report 2000-2001*. UNESCO Associated Schools Project Network in Denmark.

Byrom, J. 1999. *Minds and Machines; Britain 1750-1900*: 14-21. London: Longman.

Carey, B. 1997. *The maroon story: The authentic and original history of the maroons in the history of Jamaica, 1490-1880*. Jamaica: Agouti Press.

Caribbean Examinations Council. 1997. *The Caribbean Advanced Proficiency Examinations (CAPE) History syllabus*. St. Michael, Barbados: CXC.

Caribbean Examinations Council 2000. *Caribbean History syllabus to be examined from May/June, 2002. Secondary Education Certificate Examinations*. St. Michael, Barbados: CXC.

Child, J. 1992. *Understanding history*. London: Heinemann.

Creswell, J. W. 1998. *Qualitative inquiry and research design, choosing among five Traditions*. Thousand Oaks, CA: Sage Publications Inc.

Cross, W. E. Jr. 1998. "Black psychological functioning and the legacy of slavery: Myths and realities." In Y. Danieli (Ed.) *International handbook of multigenerational legacies of trauma*: 387-400. New York: Plenum Press

Davis, D. B. 1999. *The problem of slavery in the age of revolution 1770-1823*. Oxford, UK: Oxford University Press.

Davis, D. B. 1984. *Slavery and human progress*. Oxford, UK: Oxford University Press.

DeGruy Leary, J. 2001. "A dissertation on African American male youth violence: Trying to kill the part of you that isn't loved." PhD diss., Portland State University, Portland, OR.

Denzin, N.K. 1984. *On understanding emotion*. San Francisco: Jossey-Bass.

De Terville, D. 2002, October 13. "Repair the damage done." *The Barbados Advocate*: 21.

Deveau, J. 2001. "Towards the pedagogy of the history of the slave trade." In D.Dične (Ed.), *From chains to bonds, the slave trade revisited*: 397-415. Paris: UNESCO.

Diène, D. (Ed.). 2001. *From chains to bonds, the slave trade revisited.* Paris: UNESCO.

Dos Santos Gomes, F. 2001. "The legacy of slavery and social relations in Brazil." In G. Oostindie (Ed.), *Facing up to the past: Perspectives on the commemoration of slavery from Africa, the Americas and Europe*: 75-82. Kingston, Jamaica: Ian Randle Publishers.

Douglass, F. 2002. *Narrative of the life of an American slave.* New York: The Modern Library.

Douglass, F. 1969. *My Bondage and my freedom.* New York: Dover Publications Inc.

Douglas, S. 2002, July 21. "Eintou: The Black Pearl." *Trinidad Express, Express Woman*: 10-11.

Drescher, S. 2001. "Commemorating slavery and abolition in the United States of America." In G. Oostindie (Ed.), *Facing up to the past: Perspectives on the commemoration of slavery from Africa, the Americas and Europe*: 109-112. Kingston, Jamaica: Ian Randle Publishers.

Ejimofar, P. and J. Wilson. 2002, October 05. "No way! Resolution to expel non-Africans stays put." *Saturday Sun*: 1.

Eltis, D. 2000. *The rise of African slavery in the Americas.* Cambridge: The Press Syndicate of the University of Cambridge.

Elton, G. R. 1984. *The practice of history.* (Rev. ed). London: Fontana Paperbacks.

Gergen, M. M. and K. J. Gergen 2000. "Qualitative inquiry, tensions and transformation." In N.K. Denzin & Y.S. Lincoln (Eds.) *Handbook of qualitative research*, (2nd ed.). Thousand Oaks, CA: Sage Publications Inc.

Gift, S. 1999. *Towards a culture of peace: Teachers' use of and students' reactions to a curriculum for UNESCO associated schools.* M.Phil thesis, The University of the West Indies, St. Augustine, Trinidad and Tobago.

Goddard, S. J. 2002, October 6. "Conference poisoned by anger and hatred." *Saturday Sun*: 10A.

Goodridge, R. A. 1998. "The teaching of African history in Barbadian schools." *The Journal of Education and Development in the Caribbean.* 2 (2): 93-108.

Goleman, D. 1995. *Emotional intelligence.* New York: Bantam Books.

Goulbourne, H. 2001. "African slaves and the Atlantic world." In G. Oostindie (Ed.), *Facing up to the past: Perspectives on the commemoration of slavery from Africa, the Americas and Europe*: 127-132. Kingston, Jamaica: Ian Randle Publishers.

Gur- Ze'ev, I. 1998. "The morality of acknowledging/not-acknowledging the other's holocaust/genocide." *Journal of Moral Education, 27*(2): 161-177.

Hall, D. 1999. *In miserable slavery: Thomas Thistlewood in Jamaica*. Kingston, Jamaica: The University of the West Indies.

Hargreaves, A. 1998. "The emotional practice of teaching." *Teaching and Teacher Education*. 14 (8): 835-854.

Hector, M. and J. Casimir 2004, January 5. "Black Jacobins – Haiti's long XIX century." (E. Best & L. Best, trans). *Trinidad and Tobago Review*, 26 (1): 17-22.

Hooker, R. 1996. *The European enlightenment: seventeenth century enlightenment thought*. Retrieved January 15, 2005 from: www.wsu.edu/~dee/world.htm

Inikori, E. J. 2002. *Africans and the Industrial Revolution in England: A Study in International Trade and Economic Development*. Cambridge: Cambridge University Press.

Jacobs, H. 2000. *Incidents in the life of a slave girl*. New York: The Modern Library.

James, C.L.R. 1989. *The Black Jacobins*. (2nd ed. rev). New York: Random House Inc.

Jessop, T. S. and A. J. Penny 1999. "A story behind a story: Developing strategies for making sense of teacher narratives." *International Journal of Social Research Methodology*, Vol 2 (3): 213-230.

Khawajkie, E. 2003. "ASPnet Transatlantic Slave Trade Education Project Progress Report, 2002-2003." Paris: UNESCO

Lara, D. O. 2004. "The influence of the Haitian revolution in the Caribbean and the Americas." In *Struggles against Slavery. International Year to Commemorate the Struggle against Slavery and its Abolition*: 55. Paris: UNESCO.

Lara, D. O. 2000. "Transatlantic Slave Trade Education Project." Evaluation: *"Slave Voyages" and "Slave Voices."* Paris: UNESCO.

Lara, D. O. 1994. "Under the whiplash." *The UNESCO Courier*, October: pp 8-10.

Law, R. 2001. "The transition from the slave trade to 'Legitimate' commerce." In D. Dične (Ed.), *From chains to bonds, the slave trade revisited*: 22-35. Paris: UNESCO .

Lee, P.J. 2005. "Putting principles into practice." In M. Suzanne Donovan and John D. Bransford (Eds.), *How students learn: History in the classroom*. Washington: National Academies Press.

Levy, R. 2002. "The Transatlantic Slave Trade Education Project: An Evaluation for The Associated Schools Project Network." Division for the Promotion of Quality Education, UNESCO. University of Hertfordshire.

Lovejoy, P. E. 2000. *Transformations in slavery. A history of slavery in Africa*

(2nd ed.). Cambridge, UK: Cambridge University Press.

Maitles, H. and P. Cowan 1999. "Teaching the holocaust in primary schools in Scotland: modes, methodology and content." *Educational Review*, 51 (3): 263-271.

Marsden, W. E. 2001. *The school textbook: Geography, history and social studies.* London: Woburn Press.

Martin, T. 1993. *The Jewish onslaught. Despatches from the Wellesley battlefront.* MA, USA: The Majority Press.

Marwick, A. 1989. *The nature of history.* London: Macmillan Press Limited.

Mason, J. 1993. *Expansion, trade and industry.* London: Longman.

Matsuura, K. 2004. "Message from the Director-General of UNESCO on the occasion of the International Year to commemorate the struggle against slavery and its abolition (2004). In *Struggles against Slavery. International Year to Commemorate the Struggle against Slavery and its Abolition*: 42-43. Paris: UNESCO.

Mbembe, A. 2001. "The subject of the world." In G. Oostindie (Ed.), *Facing up to the past: Perspectives on the commemoration of slavery from Africa, the Americas and Europe*: 21-28. Kingston, Jamaica: Ian Randle Publishers.

McCaughtry, N. 2004. "The emotional dimensions of a teacher's pedagogical content knowledge: Influences on content, curriculum and pedagogy." *Journal of Teaching in Physical Education (23)* 1: 30-47.

McKenzie, J. 2003, September. "Pedagogy does matter!" *From Now On, The Educational Technology Journal, 13* (1). Retrieved November 7, 2003 from: www.fno.org/sept 03 pedagogy.html

Meredith, A. 1995. "Terry's learning: Some limitations of Shulman's pedagogical content knowledge." *Cambridge Journal of Education, 25* (2): 175-188.

Mohammed, P. 2003. "Beyond the colonised boundaries of ethnicity in Trinidad." *CLR James Journal*, 9 (1): 172-190.

Montejo, E. and M. Barnet 1993. *The autobiography of a runaway slave.* (Warwick University Caribbean Studies). (Rev. ed). London and Basingstoke: Macmillan Press Limited.

Naipaul, V.S. 2001. *The Middle Passage.* (Rev. ed). London: Macmillan Limited.

Niehaus, C. 2001. "Freedom, yes! And then what?" In G. Oostindie (Ed.), *Facing up to the past: Perspectives on the commemoration of slavery from Africa, the Americas and Europe*: 35-42. Kingston, Jamaica: Ian Randle Publishers.

Obadina, T. 2000. "Slave trade: A root of contemporary African crisis." *African Economic Analysis.* Retrieved January 6, 2003 from: www.afbis.com/analysis/slave.html

Oguibe, O. 2001. "Slavery and the diaspora imagination." In G. Oostindie (Ed.), *Facing up to the past: Perspectives on the commemoration of slavery from Africa, the Americas and Europe*: 95-101. Kingston, Jamaica: Ian Randle Publishers.

Patterson, O. 1982. *Slavery and social death, a comparative study*. London: Harvard University Press.

Ramcharitar, R. 2002, June 27. "Afrocentrism and its discontents." *The Trinidad Express*: 32-35.

Rémond, R. 1998. "History teaching and citizenship." In J. Delors (Ed.), *Education for the twenty-first century: Issues and prospects. Contributions to the work of the international commission on education for the twenty-first century*: 345-350. Paris: UNESCO.

Report of UNESCO ASPnet National Coordinators Workshop on the Implementation of the Trans-Atlantic Slave Trade (TST) Flagship Education Project "Breaking the Silence." The Gambia 23-26 April, 2001.

Richardson, L. 2000. "Writing a method of inquiry." In N. K. Denzin and Y. S. Lincoln (Eds.), *Handbook of qualitative research* (2nd ed.): 923-94. Thousand Oaks, CA: Sage Publications Inc.

Robinson, R. 2000. *The debt: What America owes to Blacks*. New York: Penguin Putnam Inc.

Rodney, W. 2000. "How Europe became the dominant section of a worldwide trade system." In V. Shepherd & H. M. Beckles (Eds.), *Caribbean slavery in the Atlantic world: A student reader*: 1-10. Kingston, Jamaica: Ian Randle Publishers.

Rosiek, J. 2003. "Emotional scaffolding. An exploration of the teacher knowledge at the intersection of student emotion and subject matter." *Journal of Teacher Education*, 54 (5): 399-412.

Sansone, L. 2001. "Remembering slavery from nearby: Heritage Brazilian style." In G. Oostindie (Ed.), *Facing up to the past: Perspectives on the commemoration of slavery from Africa, the Americas and Europe*: 83-89. Kingston, Jamaica: Ian Randle Publishers.

Sala-Molins, I. 1994. "1974: The French convention abolished slavery." *The UNESCO Courier*, October: 25.

Schmidt, N. 2004. "Against slavery: The ongoing struggle." In *Struggles against Slavery. International Year to Commemorate the Struggle against Slavery and its Abolition*: 48 61. Paris: UNESCO.

Senah, E. K. 2001. "Trinidad and the West African nexus during the nineteenth century." PhD diss., The University of the West Indies, St. Augustine Trinidad and Tobago.

Shepard, L. 2000. "The role of assessment in a learning culture." *Educational Researcher*, 29 (7): 1-14

Shepherd, V. A. 2000. "Image representation and the project of emancipation: History and identity in the commonwealth Caribbean." In. K. Hall & D. Benn (Eds.), *Contending with destiny: The Caribbean in the 21st century*: 53-57. Kingston, Jamaica: Ian Randle Publishers.

Sherwood, M. 1998. "Sins of omission and commission: History in English schools and struggles for change." *Multicultural Teaching*: 14-23.

Shulman, L. S. 1987. "Knowledge and teaching: Foundations of the new reform." *Harvard Educational Review 57* (1): 1-22.

Small, J. 2003, June 14. "African philosophy and the challenges in the 21st century." *Newsday*: 9.

Soglo, N. 2001. Foreword in D. Dične (Ed.), *From chains to bonds, the slave trade revisited*: xii-xv. Paris: UNESCO.

Soumonni, E. 2001, February. "The impact of the transatlantic slave trade on interethnic relations in contemporary Africa." Public lecture, Mona Campus, The University of the West Indies, Jamaica.

Stampp, K. 1971. "Rebels and sambos: The search for the negro's personality in slavery." *Journal of Southern History, xxxvii*: 367-392.

Tatum, D. B. 1999. *Why are all the black kids sitting together in the cafeteria? And other conversations about race*. New York: Basic Books.

Tatum, D.B. 1992. "Talking about race, learning about racism: The application of racial identity development theory in the classroom." *Harvard Educational Review 62* (1): 1-24.

UNESCO 2002. "The Dakar framework for action, education for all: Meeting our collective commitments." Paris: UNESCO.

UNESCO Associated Schools Project Network, 1998, August. "Triangular Transatlantic Slave Route Education Flagship Project: Report of Meeting of International Task Force." Port-au-Prince, Haiti.

UNESCO. "The ASPnet Transatlantic Slave Trade Education Project: Breaking the Silence. The Slave Route." Paris: UNESCO.

UNESCO. 1996. "Learning: The treasure within: Report to UNESCO of the International Commission on Education for the Twenty-first Century." Paris: UNESCO.

Vaswani, R. 2001. "A respectable trade." In G. Oostindie (Ed.), *Facing up to the past: Perspectives on the commemoration of slavery from Africa, the Americas and Europe*: 138-143). Kingston, Jamaica: Ian Randle Publishers.

Walvin, J. 1993. *Black ivory: A history of British slavery*. London: Fontana Press.

Williams, E. 1944. *Capitalism and Slavery*. London: The University of North Carolina Press.

# Index

A perception of the human tragedy of the TTEA as continuing today, 159
Abbé Raynal, 12
Abolitionists, 6
Accumulation of capital for the financing of the Industrial Revolution, 6
Achille Mbembe, 22
Adam Smith, 12
Africa contributed to the development of Western Europe, 9
Africa: Benin, Senegal, the Gambia, 69, 71, 97
African American students' increased capacity for empathy, 159
African Americans largely overwhelmed by a majority culture, 46 ***
African diaspora, 23, 26, 114, 117, 182
African enslavement, 3, 114
African enslavement for western progress, 6
African refusal to face up to its own responsibility in the TTEA, 24
African-Caribbean self-disparagement, 34
Africans enslaved by France, 12
Africans in Western Europe in the 18th Century, 84, 99, 106
Africans participated in the enslavement of their own people, 147
Africa's loss of skill and potential development, 105
Afrocentrism, 115
Age of Enlightenment, 11, 38
Aleauria, 94
Alex Hayley, 15, 20

Allison Blakely, 22, 25
Ama Ata Aidoo, 22
American beliefs about slavery, 18 not black history but American history, 140
American history not black history, 140
American national demographics, 27
American tendency to turn a blind eye, 27
American understanding of slavery, 118
Amerinidans and indentured labourers from India, 41
Amistad, 15, 126, 146, 161
Amnesty International, 63
Anansi stories, 33
Antiracist educators - USA, 30
Anti-slavery advocates, 12
Appreciating the value of knowing one's ancestry, 139
Arab slave trade, 10, 22
Arthur Marwick, 1
Associated Schools Project Network (ASPnet), viii, 18, 42, 115
Avoidance of the subject of racism, 31
Bailyn, 19
Beverly Tatum, 4, 30
Black American culture, 21
Black Atlantic, 11
Black holocaust, 10
Black people's identity and self-esteem, 32
Black people's internalization of the racist message, 33
Black people's self-degradation, 26
Black Power, 139
Black slavery - a fatal incentive, 6

Blackburn, 9
Boyer, 93
Brazil, 24
Brazilian economy built on the shoulders of the slave, 123
Brion David Davis, 5
Britain's collective national consciousness about slavery, 14
Britain's role, 107
Burden of blackness, 36
Businesslike principles, 19
Bussa, 40, 91, 94
C.L.R. James, 8, 93, 131
Caifazes, 93
Capitalist development, 6
Capoeira, 91, 118
Caribbean Advanced Proficiency Examination (CAPE), 75
Carrington, 8
Case Study Approach, 65
Cateau, 8
Categories of slave labour, 83, 98
Celebrating positive contributions of Africans, 114
Celebration of national heroes and heroines, 40
Cessation of the trade, 103
Challenges of teaching the TTEA, 136
Charles de Secondat, 11
Chattel enslavement, 20
Christopher Columbus, 115
Civil rights in Europe, 12
Civil rights movement statutes, 26
Clandestine trade, 100
Classical economists, 6
Clarkson, 14
Colin Palmer, 9
Collective memory, 20
Colonial relationships continue in the Caribbean, 40
Colonization and apartheid, 22
Communicating the humanity of the enslaved Africans, 114
Concept of the racial inferiority of Africans, 28
Connecting, journal writing, poetry and artistic expression, 118

Conspiracy of silence, 24
Constraints of the national curriculum, 113
Constructive emotion, 58
Contemporary black problems, 30
Contemporary negative black birthing and marriage patterns, 30
Content knowledge, 52
Continuation of the legacy of slavery - USA, 26
Conveyors of negativity, 30
Criteria for enslavement today, 7
Creoles, 94
Cross's (1991) Model of Black Identity Development, 32
Cultural legacies of the trade, 118, 124
Cultural racism, 30
Cultural transformation, 4
Cutback on the slave trade, 104
CXC, ix, 7, 74
Daniel Goleman, 56
David Blight, 20
Death of any sense of cultural ownership, 29
Defenders of apartheid in South Africa, 15
Dehumanization of the African, 84
Demand for labour, 2
Denial and lack of interest on the part of students, 155
Denmark - general educational concept, 68
Dessalines, 93
Deveau, 15
Developed economic rationalization of the system, 5
Development of ideas within European capitalist society, 2
Dialectical relationship between development and underdevelopment, 9
Discomfort of white teachers, 32
Discovering the contributions of Africans, 158
Dismantling of the colonial system, 38
Distribution of jobs by gender, 106
Dominant group, 32

Doudou Diène, 15
Duration of the TTEA, 87, 99, 108
Earl Lovelace, 37
Effects of ties with Africa, 2
Eintou Springer, 36
Elisée Soumonni, 23
Emmanuel Kwaku Senah, 35
Emotional Responses of Non-African Students in Barbados and Trinidad and Tobago, 157
Emotional dimensions, 145
English-speaking Caribbean, 33
Enlightenment thought, 1, 41, 114
Enslaved Africans - central part of the American economy, 11
Enslaved Africans resistance during the journey, 102
Enslaved Africans considered part of the family, 98
Enslaved not slaves, 3
Enslaved persons are still being traded, 88
Enslavement of Africans by Europeans was necessary, 13
Eric Williams, 3, 6, 7, 131
Establishing the Relevance of the TTEA, 132
Ethnic jokes, 30
Ethno-racial politics in Brazil, 25
Eunuchs, 98
European capitalist development, 6
Europe: England, Denmark, 105
Europe's trade connection with Africa, 2
Europeans see the African as sub-human, 96
Evangelical Christian abolitionists, 6
Exorcism of slavery - Brazil, 24
Factors impacting on teachers' delivery of content knowledge, 132
Features of Caribbean civilization, 35
Features of slavery, 5
Findings of the Project Evaluation, 76
Flávio dos Santos Gomes, 22
Focusing on strength of enslaved Africans, 162
Force of the whip, 23
Francisco de Miranda, 38

Frederick Douglass, 115, 129
Frederick Engels, 6
Free labour superior to enslaved labour, 12
Free womb law, 94
French Revolution, 12, 93
Generation of black Europeans, 182
George Lamming, 37
Gert Oostindie, 22
Gilder Lehrman Institute of American History, 18
Haitian culture, 21
Haitian Revolution, 38, 93
Harriet Beecher Stowe, 17
Harry Goulbourne, 13, 33, 39, 182
Heavy silence about TTEA, 16
Hector and Casimir, 38
Heritage Week, 92, 128
Hilary McD. Beckles, 3, 22, 33, 45
Historiography, 1, 6, 19, 44, 64, 176
How enslaved Africans were used, 83, 97, 100, 106
How individuals were captured and sold, 97
Image contamination of Haiti, 39
Immigration, 94
Impact of teaching methodology, 148
Importance of teachers' knowledge, 133
Inadequate time for research and for teaching, 137
Inadequate transparency and accessibility of the study of Africa and slavery, 36
Inclusion of factual information about the trade in school curricula, 16
Industrial Revolution, 2, 6, 103, 107
Inhumanity of the auction sale, 185
Insights for Teaching the TTEA, 165
Institutionalized racism, 30
Interpretation of the trade, 8
Invisibility and inequality - Brazil, 24
Involvement of Africans in the TTEA, 115
Issues and challenges, 64
James Horton, 11, 21
James Walvin, 15, 22
Jerry Rosiek, 50, 173

John Blassingame, 130
John Creswell, 65
John Jacob Thomas, 8
John Millar, 6
John T. Brue, 51
Joy DeGruy Leary, 28
Karl Marx, 5, 6
Kevin Bales, 7
Kids to Africa, 128
King Christophe, 84
Knowledge of American history, 18
Koïchiro Matsuura, 9, 37
l'esclaverie, 98
Lack of information about the achievements of oppressed groups, 30
Lack of respect for dark skinned people, 34
Large international corporations, 7
Lee Shulman's, 69
Legacies and human development, 13
Legacies of slavery, 1, 12, 26, 34, 112, 139
Legacy of negativity, 96
Legal paternity, 5
Livio Sansone, 10, 22
Lloyd Best, 34
Lorrie Shepard, 50
Major slave trading ports, 87, 99, 108
Major sources for the teaching knowledge base, 52
Margaret Mitchell, 17
Marie-Jean-Antoine-Nicolas de Caritat, 11
Marika Sherwood, 13
Maroons, 90, 102, 110
Marronage, 91, 102, 110, 128
Marsden, 114
Marwick, 113
Mary Abbot, 1
Marxist writers, 14
Master-slave relationship, 4
Memorialization of the TTEA, 1, 13
Memory and History, 19, 21, 31
Mental slavery, 96
Michael Manley, 8
Middle Passage, 10, 20, 26, 36, 73, 89, 100, 109, 114, 127, 152, 173
Modern day slavery, 7, 8, 100
Modern scholars, 9
Moral debt, 13, 15, 18
Mortality rate, 89
Multidisciplinary approach to teaching TTEA, 117
Myth of passivity, 116
Nanny, leader of a Jamaican Maroon clan, 40
Nate McCaughtry, 50
Nation states emerging from plantations, 40
Negotiations with African slave dealers, 97
Nelly Schmidt, 2, 11
Nicéphore Soglo, 33
Nomenclaturing, 114
NORAD, 19, 44
Objectives of the ASPnet TST Education Project, 43
Olaudah Equiano, 106
Olu Oguibe, 10, 22, 33
Opening up of the New World for wealth generation, 3
Opportunities for teaching black history, 134
Oral data, 23
Organisation for African Unity, 15
Orlando Patterson, 4
Overcoming hardship, 115
Paradigm of victimization, 22
Passive racism, 31
Patricia Mohammed, 35
Paul Bogle, 40
Paul Lovejoy, 4
Pedagogical content knowledge, 51
Perceptions of Caribbean people of their history, 9
Perspective of contemporary researchers and writers, 22
Phillip Curtin, 130
Places of Memory, 104, 123, 128, 140, 173
Plantations, 5, 83, 86, 98, 106
Poor self-image of youths of African ancestry, ix

Portugal, 86, 99
Post-Graduate Certificate of Education, 134
Post Traumatic Slave Syndrome, 28
Preferential treatment of persons of lighter complexion, 139
Problematic and flawed social construct, 4, 19
Process of emergence, 41
Process of enslavement, 3
Production of staple commodities for global trade, 5
Profits from slavery, 2
Promoting intercultural dialogue, 162
Psychological persuasion, 4
Public school curricula, 7
Published research works and their impact on school and university curricula, 23
Quakers, 103
Quilombos, 24, 91, 115
Race in the USA in the 21$^{st}$ century, 17
Race related memories, 50
Racial categories, 4
Racism in America is institutionalized, 31
Racism is a contradiction of justice, 31
Randall Robinson, 9
Rate of exploitation of the enslaved Africans, 9
Rebellion of the enslaved Africans in Santo Domingo, 38
Recommendations for teaching the TTEA, 179
Reformed vision of curriculum, 59, 175
Religious bodies, 103
René Rémond, 61
Reparations debate, 15, 182
Research and reason to reconstruct the past; 21
Revised mandatory national curriculum in history, 14
Revisionist works on slavery, 36
Revolts by enslaved Africans on board the ships, 101
Richard Goodridge, 33
Richard Hooker, 41

Rise of racism, 3
Rise of seaport towns in Europe, 2
Robinson, 15, 21, 26, 182
Roger Levy, 49
Sam Sharpe, 40
Samuel Prescod, 40
Sarah Gill, 40
Scaffolding, 57, 173
Schoelcher, 47
School and the curriculum, 13
Segregation and racial discrimination - USA, 10
Selection phase of pedagogical reasoning and action, 54
Sexagenarian law, 94
Sexual abuse of enslaved Africans, 98
Seymour Drescher, 22
Shepherd and Beckles, 3,
Shirley Gordon, 131
Shortcoming of pedagogical content knowledge theory and research, 57
Shulman's (1987) model of pedagogical reasoning and action, 53
Significant observations of the UNESCO survey, 46
Silence about the TTEA trade, 15
Silence in Africa, 24
Simon Bolivar, 38
Skilled teaching, 51
Skin bleaching, 34
Slave owner, 4
Slave ships crossing the Atlantic, 89, 101, 109
Slave traders, 97, 109
Slave type relations today, 109
Slavery, 10
Slavery as a long established idea, 114
Slavery existed in Africa, 86
Slavery has not ended, 7
Slavery in American history, 27
Slavery in Brazil, 84, 99, 106
Slavery reintroduced after the French Revolution, 111
Slavery, a progressive institution, 6
Slavery's role in the promotion of racial prejudice and ideology, 3
Social categorization, 4

Social death, 23
Social justice through citizenship, 40
Social non-person, 4
Social theorists, 6
Socialization of the enslaved, 117 Spain, 86, 99
Stanley Oaken, 130
Strategies for teaching the TTEA, 91
Strengthening of teacher knowledge, 179
Student segregation, 156
Students appreciating different perspectives on history, 139
Students' awareness of the legacies of the TTEA, 156
Students' psychological responses to race-related content, 31
Summary of some resources used by teachers for the TTEA survey, 131
Supply of enslaved Africans to the New World, 82, 97, 105
Survey of students' knowledge and attitudes on the TTEA, 44
Survivor syndromes, 29
Symbolic remorse - USA, 25
Tabula rasa of Africa, 13
Taking students out of the classroom, 123
Teacher development and teachers sharing their experiences, 135
Teacher expertise, 165, 168, 177
Teacher training, 134
Teachers' emotions, 149, 159
Teachers' knowledge, interest and passion, 132
Teachers' objectivity and balance, 147
Teachers' poor self-image, 139
Teaching of African history in Barbados, 32
Teaching resources, 126
Teaching strategies Employed, 117
Textbooks, 18, 37, 75, 77, 130, 136, 180
The Africans' resistance to being captured in Africa, 36
The Americas/Caribbean: Brazil, 73
The Americas/Caribbean: New Orleans, the United States of America, 72
The Americas/Caribbean: The Dominican Republic, 75
The Americas/Caribbean: The English-speaking Caribbean – Barbados, Jamaica, Trinidad and Tobago, 74
The arts and cultural manifestations, 117
The case of an African-Caribbean identity crisis, 35
The emotional dimension of teaching, 82, 171
The enslaved and the enslavers, 114
The essence of history, 21
The exploitation of Africa, 107
The four pillars of education, 61
The Gate of No Return, 104
The human tragedy of the TTEA, 95, 104
The issue of human development, 41
The new slavery, 7
The New World, 3
The omission or lack of attention paid to the TTEA in classroom teaching, 68
The parliamentary plan, 93
The principal symbol of the suffering of black people historically, 22
The role of European countries in the Trade, 85, 99, 107, 157
The term, enslaved, 3
The trauma-transcendence legacy model, 29
The Tree of Forgetting, 105
The Triangular Slave Trade, 85, 99, 107, 125
The United Kingdom - general education concept, 66
The violence of slavery, 4
Theories relating to slavery and economic progress, 5
Thomas Clarkson, 12
Three facets of the power relation, 4
Today's enslaved persons, 7
Toni Morrison, 15
Toussaint L'Ouverture, 92, 103, 114
Transition of societies from violence to

the rule of law, 61
Transnational phenomenon, 11
Trauma and institutionalized racism –
  the African American situation, 28
TTEA an emotive and difficult topic to
  teach, 146
TTEA as a phenomenon in world
  history, 8
TTEA as a turning point for the
  prosperity of Europe, 107
Tumbeiro, 90
Twentieth-century American law and
  custom assumptions of white
  supremacy, 18
Twi language, 128
Types of bias and prejudice, 78
UK history textbooks, 14
Umbanda, 25
Unconstructive emotions, 58
Underground Railroad, 26
Understanding the classroom's social
  dynamics, 57
UNDP Human Development Report
  (1995), 60
UNESCO, viii, 5, 8, 105
UNESCO Associated Schools
  'Transatlantic Slave Trade Education
  Project', viii, 42, 181
Universal Declaration of Human Rights,
  43
Use of racial ideologies, 5
Use or threat of violence, 4
Value judgements in the teaching of
  history, 62
Valuing people of African descent and
  acts of resistance, 115
Verene Shepherd, 34
Voltaire, 12
Vygotsky, 57, 173
Walter Rodney, 2, 9, 12, 37
Walvin, 27, 182
Wellman's (1977) definition of racism,
  30
Western Europe contributed to Africa's
  underdevelopment, 9
White racism, 3
White standards of beauty, 34

Why the slave trade to the Caribbean
  was stopped, 93, 103, 111
William Cross, 29, 162
William Gordon, 40
William Wilberforce, 12, 14, 47
Yael Danieli, 29
Young African American students and
  racism, 32
Youths of non-European heritage in the
  British school system, 13

www.ingramcontent.com/pod-product-compliance
Lightning Source LLC
Chambersburg PA
CBHW070648160426
43194CB00009B/1627